YOUR LIFE'S WORK

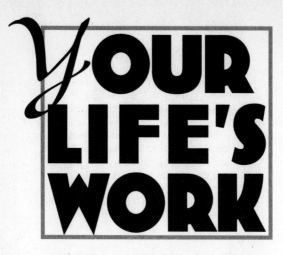

YOUR LIFE'S WORK

A GUIDE TO CREATING A SPIRITUAL AND SUCCESSFUL WORK LIFE

Tami Coyne

BERKLEY BOOKS, NEW YORK

Kind permission was granted to reprint the following:
"A Journey Through the Mist" by Nicholas Gaudiuso, page 1,
previously published in *The Ebbing Tide*, by The National Library of Poetry;
Untitled by Michael Mannion, page 27;
"You Are the Light" by Peter Schaufele, page 93;
Untitled by Miroslaw Kucharski, page 225.

This book is an original publication of The Berkley Publishing Group.

YOUR LIFE'S WORK

A Berkley Book / published by arrangement with
the author

PRINTING HISTORY
Berkley trade paperback edition / April 1998

The Penguin Putnam Inc. World Wide Web site address is
http://www.penguinputnam.com

ISBN: 0-425-16162-5

BERKLEY®
Berkley Books are published by The Berkley Publishing Group,
a member of Penguin Putnam Inc.,
200 Madison Avenue, New York, New York 10016.
BERKLEY and the "B" design
are trademarks belonging to Berkley Publishing Corporation.

PRINTED IN THE UNITED STATES OF AMERICA

10 9 8 7 6 5 4 3 2 1

THIS BOOK IS DEDICATED TO
ALL SEEKERS ON THE PATH

AND TO

DR. ALFRED A. KAYATA, JACKIE KAYATA, AND MARY MANTI,
WITHOUT WHOM MANY SEEKERS MIGHT NOT
HAVE FOUND THEIR WAY.

ACKNOWLEDGMENTS

I would like to thank the following people without whom this book would not have been possible: Giuseppe Scorcia, for being the love of my life; Michael Mannion, for his support, love, and friendship, and for the gift of allowing me to publish his beautiful poem; Nicholas Gaudiuso, for his radiant personality and for "A Journey Into the Mist"; Peter Schaufele, for the gifts of music, love, and "You Are the Light"; Miroslaw Kucharski, for his loving heart and for his remarkable poem; Claire Gerus, for being an angelic messenger of the divine; Regula Noetzli, for being a great literary agent and a true agent of Spirit; Jennifer Lata, Judith Palais, and The Berkley Publishing Group, for making *Your Life's Work* a reality; Shawn Coyne, my brother, for his counsel and for his belief in me when I needed it the most; Bibb Bailey, for her support and encouragement; Teri Coyne, my sister, for always believing in me and for her illuminating insight into that thing we call life; Pat Coyne, my brother, Beth Wagner

Coyne, and Sara Delaney Coyne, for a brave new beginning; Mary Joan Coyne, my mother, for traveling the spiritual road with me and for loving me unconditionally; Patrick Coyne, my father, for supporting and encouraging my ventures into the un-known; Rosemary Hayden, my aunt, for being a living Soul; Mary Ann Coyne, my aunt, for her courage; Jack O'Malley, my cousin, for the example of his life; the Scorcia and Gaudiuso families—Chiara, Joanne, Sante, Nancy, Carina, Jon, Annie, Pie-tro, Maria, Nico, and Tonia—for their love; Kristin Martin, Julia Davis, Cara Alongi McDonough, Brian McDonough, Stephanie Ackler, Peter Chapin, Lydia Lawson, Lucinda Lormier, Anne Brenner, Debra Buck, Adrianne Weingarten, Alexandra Lenes Kaufman, Phyllis Clements, and Barbara and Stanley Parris, for the gift of true friendship; Deborah Boughner, for helping me to find my path; the Brooklyn Beam Club, for keeping me on the path; and finally, all those people whose stories became part of this book—thank you for showing the way home.

CONTENTS

INTRODUCTION

This book you are holding in your hands is unusual. It is unusual because it is the result of both my philosophical inquiry into the relationship between spirituality and work and my day-to-day experience working "in the trenches." Unlike other authors who have written on this subject, I am not a well-known expert in the field. I do not hold a degree in theology or science, nor do I have a Ph.D. in psychology, counseling, or social work. I am simply a person, like yourself, who has always known that there is more to life than meets the eye and has always yearned to live a happy, productive, prosperous, and successful life.

My interest in spirituality was first piqued by the religious training that I received as a child. Even though this training gave me a glimpse into the unknown, a further study of traditional Western religious dogma couldn't provide me with a satisfactory answer to the questions Who am I? and Why am I here? And while I was intrigued with Eastern philosophy, I couldn't afford to head off to the Himalayas in search of cosmic truth. In addition, while I had no desire to pursue science as a career, I knew that for the most part I accepted the validity of its findings. By the time I was a young adult, my philosophical dilemma centered around how to reconcile theology and science in some meaningful way.

By the time I graduated from college, however, my philosophical dilemma had taken a practical turn. I now needed to be able to find a way to make enough money to support myself while I continued to try to find out why I was here on planet Earth and what I was meant to do with my life. This desire led me to many different jobs and a few different careers. It also led me to question many of the assumptions I had about the nature of work, about my own nature, and about the nature of the universe itself. Eventually, when my desire for knowledge outweighed my ability to withstand the pain and suffering of not living the life I wanted to live, I was miraculously led to a chiropractic office in Brooklyn, New York. It was here that I was introduced to Dr. Alfred A. Kayata, an exceptional healer and metaphysics teacher, and to a little-known course of study called Concept-Therapy®.

Concept-Therapy® is the brainchild of Dr. Thurman Fleet, a chiropractor who was born in 1895 and died in 1983. Although I never met Dr. Fleet, I am told that he was an amazingly courageous and loving human being who, despite many obstacles, was relentless in his search for Truth. After a peak experience in 1931, Dr. Fleet developed a practical and workable philosophy of life that correlates the teachings of religion with the findings of science, and a course of study intended to provide a method of attaining cosmic consciousness.

Needless to say, I have been deeply influenced and inspired by Dr. Fleet's work, as well as by Dr. Kayata, whose interpretation of the work and original insight into the nature of reality have been among the greatest gifts of my life. *Your Life's Work*, however, is the result of my own evolving and personal quest for the answers to life's mysteries. Any mistakes I may have made are due to my own limited vision and are in no way a reflection of Concept-Therapy®.

I only hope that the themes I develop in this book serve in some small way to pay homage to Dr. Fleet, who did what he did not for personal gratification or reward, but simply because it was his job to do it, and to Dr. Kayata, Jackie Kayata, and Mary Manti, my teachers and my friends.

I urge anyone interested in walking the spiritual path to get involved in Concept-Therapy®. The rewards are immeasurable. For more information, call the Concept-Therapy® Institute at (800) 531-5628; visit their web site at http://www.concept-therapy.org; or write them at 25550 Boerne Stage Road, San Antonio, Texas 78255-9585.

PART ONE

THE MAP IS NOT THE TERRITORY

A JOURNEY THROUGH THE MIST

Do you understand the rain?
See it bless or does it stain?
On this brisk November night,
enter into its domain.
Release your hold; contemplate;
recall the past; envision fate.
Shining through the darkened light,
feel emotions it creates.
It trickles down the windowside,
like tears you know you just can't hide.
The pain is blind, so close your eyes,
do not fear and fear's denied.
Rain's severe, embrace the sun,
your mind and body have joined as one.
Rise above and hurt no more,
for now your freedom has begun.

—NICHOLAS GAUDIUSO

Apparently no one is exempt from the dreaded buzzwords of the nineties: downsizing and restructuring. The great majority are not free from the anxiety and panic that result when a job held one day may or may not exist the next. Who will survive and flourish in these times of uncertainty?

The people who are ultimately seen as trailblazers and success stories are the ones who, driven by trying circumstances, realize that adaptation is the key to evolution. These individuals see latent opportunity during times of transformation, confront and challenge their outmoded beliefs about "how things really work," and regain the control over their own lives that they once so willingly handed over to the almighty powers that be. Once in the driver's seat, these individuals are no longer willing to return to being passengers who are simply along for the ride.

Each one of us has the potential to be a trailblazer and a success story—regardless of our sex, class, educational level, or age—and it is our spiritual power that is the key to this success. It is not a coincidence that cultural and economic transformation is occurring at the same time that interest in spirituality is growing by leaps and bounds. Seen in its true light, the entire transformation is the result of the process of spiritual unfolding that is at the core of our development as a species. We are renewing our bond with the Spirit within and are slowly awakening from the spiritual slumber that has lasted for centuries.

Signs of this awakening are everywhere. Once the slaves of established dogma—political, economic, and religious—Americans in large numbers are now seeking alternative ways of understanding the situations with which they are confronted, as well as the world as a whole. Spirituality, once solely the domain of priests, ministers, rabbis, and other religious leaders, is now becoming an individual matter. As we shift from an industrial to an informational economy, we are also shifting from a culture that sees God as out there somewhere to a culture that feels God is somewhere inside us. The darkness that has enshrouded us for generations is slowly being replaced by the light of heightened self-awareness. The recognition dawns that we have not been forsaken by God, that we do not need to give up our power as individuals in return for security, that we have the ability to satisfy all of our own needs and to transform our personal and work lives into soulful expressions of our true spiritual nature.

This is an exciting time to be alive. The new science and the perennial spiritual philosophy at the heart of most, if not all, religious systems have converged. Both science and theology, while using different terminology, are in agreement on one main point. Science tells us that everything in the material world is simply a manifestation of energy. Science sometimes defines energy as synonymous with consciousness—that is, the intelligence inherent in energy that knows what it is supposed to do—from creating a molecule all the way up to forming the systems that make up our bodies and beyond. Theology tells us the same thing, but replaces the term "energy" with the term "Spirit" or "God." Regardless of whether we use science or theology as a road map for our discussion, the question that arises is: What does this concept mean insofar as the individual is concerned?

In simple terms, it means that we are not who we think we are, not simply a body with a brain/mind that works like an advanced computer processing unit. Since energy/consciousness or Spirit/God is all that really exists, all of us have been created from, and are composed of, this mysterious essence. Therefore, we are not separate and discrete entities disconnected from the universe, from each other, and from our ultimate source. We are not servants of our economy or our culture, but rather we are masters of our own destiny. Each one of us is an individual manifestation of this one great life, regardless of what name we use to describe it. Each one of us is literally a god in the making— with all the responsibility that goes along with such a distinction.

Our current dilemma is the result of one thing and one thing only—an erroneous understanding of who we truly are. Science can help us to understand certain aspects of our place in the grand scheme of things but cannot answer the existential and philosophical questions that surface in the wee hours of the morning before dawn distracts us with the demands of a new day. We dimly remember from our religious training, if we had any, that we have a soul, but what exactly does this mean, and where is this soul actually located? We know on some level that it is this soul that connects us to our source—Spirit or God—but what we seem to have forgotten is that because we are manifestations of Spirit, and were created from Spirit, we are, in the final analysis, spiritual beings. As spiritual beings, we do not have souls, we *are* living Souls. As living Souls, our only job is to realize our full potential as co-creators with our divine source and to act as agents of the ultimate good.

These notions of Spirit and Soul are all well and good on the theoretical level, but what practical value exists in all of this? How are we to act as Souls when science cannot prove that such a thing exists? Even if we take it on faith that we are spiritual beings with the capacity to act as agents of the ultimate good, how are we supposed to go about doing this in the workplace, where survival of the fittest is the name of the game and getting ahead means exhibiting the tried and true emotions of selfishness and greed?

The answer is not as elusive as it may seem. But before it can be answered, a further understanding of ourselves as spiritual and material beings is required.

The fight between traditional science and religion has always centered around whether humans are material or spiritual beings. The basic premise of this book is that we are both at the same time. We are material beings because we have brains/minds and bodies, and we are spiritual beings because we are Souls who are infused with Spirit. Because we are both material and spiritual beings, the two dimensions are inextricably linked. In fact, the material realm of existence is simply Spirit manifesting itself in physical form.

There is no great mystery surrounding what constitutes the material dimension. Our bodies occupy space within it, our senses recognize it, and our emotions react to it. The spiritual dimension is more difficult to pin down because most of us are the heirs of the scientific worldview which questions and doubts anything that cannot be measured and analyzed in a laboratory. We are also the heirs, however, of the belief held by many philosophers and religious teachers that the spiritual dimension is not located somewhere in the heavens, but is here now, within us. The dilemma that has faced many a spiritual seeker is how to access this dimension and how to use the knowledge that comes as a result.

There are as many ways to access the spiritual dimension as there are individuals, but all of these methods have one thing in common: They all use either the mind or the body to bypass ordinary sensual reality in an effort to merge with the spiritual dimension or the ground of being. Because this is first and foremost a book about the relationship between spirituality and work, rather than a book about the relationship between spirituality and sports, we will concentrate our attention on that organ of the body that separates us from the rest of the creatures of the world: our brains/minds.

Everyone knows that the brain is a complex organ that regulates our bodies and receives and reacts to sensory stimulation from the outside world. The definition of the mind, however, is more nebulous. Because it is not an organ separate from the brain, it must be considered as part of the function of the brain or as the activity of the brain. The mind is the seat of our self-awareness and our self-consciousness. It responds to occurrences in the outside world through whatever emotion it reasons is appropriate based on past experiences.

Our ability to think inwardly, to reason, is what separates us from other living creatures. An animal goes about its daily activity guided by instinct. It does not question its place in the universe, complain that it must find food for itself, or wonder which of its fellow animals it should take as its mate. It is completely ruled by primitive urges, paramount of which is the urge for self-preservation. In other words, the animal, who has a brain but not a mind as we understand it, is completely taken care of by the infinite wisdom of nature and does not have the ability to choose.

As infants, we are not that far removed from the animal. We do not yet know that we are a separate being within the vast ocean of life. We are completely guided by Spirit as we develop into beings who can think inwardly. The innate intelligence within, along with the care and nurturing of our parents, takes care of all our needs.

I recently experienced a magnificent example of how innate intelligence or Spirit is at work in an infant. During an overnight visit with my beautiful one month-old niece, Sara, her mother told me that she was concerned that her baby, like most newborns, was suffering from colic and gas. My brother and sister-in-law warned me that I would hear a lot of crying during the night and prepared me for the worst. The next morning, I remarked that I was surprised that I had not even heard a peep out of Sara during the night. My sister-in-law told me that the weirdest thing had occurred. It seems that Sara, who usually nursed every four hours and then suffered with gas, decided with no prodding from her mother to eat smaller amounts every two hours. For the first time, she was experiencing only minor gas.

As I looked into the eyes of this wondrous creature, I was in awe that such a small infant, who had not yet developed the ability to think inwardly or to reason, was guided by some invisible force, directing her how to correct her painful condition. I realized that if Sara's needs were being taken care of by this invisible power, it was only logical that nature, energy, or Spirit would not forsake those of us who through the maturation process had acquired a higher mental ability.

This higher mental ability begins to take hold when the child develops self-awareness. When a human being recognizes for the first time that he or she is a separate individual and learns that he or she can manipulate his or her external environment, the inner life of the mind develops, and the ability to reason emerges. With the emergence of self-consciousness and reason, the human develops more and more complex emotions, especially fear.

What is the reason for this deep-seated emotion? The answer is not that difficult to understand. In the animal kingdom, from which the human kingdom has evolved, the self-preservation instinct is very strong. Fear, in effect, is nature's way of alerting the animal to potential danger. The animal is not self-conscious and is totally reliant on instinct to make the decision whether to confront the danger or flee. In other words, the animal feels fear as an instinctive response to danger, but, unaware that it is alive or even an entity separate from its surroundings, it does not fear death itself.

On the other hand, the human is still influenced by the self-preservation urge, but thanks to self-consciousness and reason, he or she has the power to choose how to respond to danger. At the same time, however, the human also feels the emotion of fear more powerfully knowing that his or her decision could result in extinction, in death.

Fear, then, is the result of feeling separated from our source, from nature, God, or Spirit, and of recognizing the reality and inevitability of physical death. As a consequence of this overwhelming fear, on the deepest of levels we believe that the universe in which we live is not inherently good, that all is not well with the world. To make matters worse, our parents, even though they raised us in the best way they could, more often than not instilled the same fears in us that were instilled in them: fear of failure, fear of death, fear of disease, fear of injury, fear of other people, fear of life itself.

In fact, our whole culture is based on fear. We believe more in the power of evil than we do in the power of good. Just turn on the evening news or read the newspaper if you need to see the power that evil has over our lives. For every story about the power of good, there are a hundred that remind us we are not safe, secure, and loved. We have become a culture of victims, victims of our own fear.

This is not to say that evil does not exist or that bad things do not happen. We perpetrate the evil over and over every day, however, by focusing all of our attention on it and never giving "good" equal time. The result of such victimhood is slavery. We are the slaves of an outmoded worldview that wreaks havoc on the planet by turning self-aware, mentally able human beings into sheep who are afraid of their own shadow for fear that something bad will happen. As sheep, we only have recourse to the tried and true emotions of greed, worry, anger, criticism, jealousy, and hatred.

In the 1980s, we witnessed the actor Michael Douglas, in the movie *Wall Street,* portraying an egomaniacal power-broker who proclaimed that "Greed is good," a phrase that came to symbolize all that was negative about the decade. Crazed powerbrokers not-withstanding, most people find the emotion of greed to be ob-jectionable, to say the least, but rarely wonder how and why they express this emotion. Further, they rarely question what this emo-tion truly signifies.

Greed is the appropriate response to a belief that there is not enough to go around and that we will not get our fair share. This belief is easy to understand given the fact that we have all been indoctrinated, consciously or not, by the economic principle of scarcity. Fear of not having enough manifests itself in the selfish desire for more than is needed, and in the endless exploitation of our natural resources and our fellow human beings. As objectionable as it is, greed is currently one of the most prevalent of our emotions as a species.

I await the day that worry becomes an Olympic sport, given its tremendous popularity. Although worry is not considered nearly as objectionable as greed, it does severely hamper productive activity. When I first began a serious study of the negative emotions, I tried to count how often a worrisome thought entered my head. After about ten minutes I gave up. *What if I lose my job? What if my child doesn't make friends on his first day of kindergarten? What if I get cancer?* What if, what if, what if . . . It is no mystery that worry is the fear that bad things will happen or that we will not be able to handle the situations we encounter on a daily basis. It is also not a mystery that people who engage in this great pastime are frequently, if not constantly, anxious and apprehensive. It is as if there is a neverending tape running in our minds constantly reminding us to be on guard, not to relax, to fear the future. If we fear the future, however, what power do we have in the present to avoid the things we are worrying about?

Worry is also the result of trying to be absolutely perfect every minute of every day. I had just graduated from college and, after much worrying, landed a job as a legal assistant in a prestigious Wall Street law firm. I desperately wanted to be the perfect employee. One day a partner in the firm gave me an assignment. He told me that it was an incredibly important project, that he needed the work done in two days, and that I couldn't make any mistakes because it was for a major client. I went home that night and spent about seven straight hours worrying that I couldn't do the job. I went in the next day and somehow completed the assignment, despite the fact that I was a nervous wreck. That evening, I was exhausted from my emotional turmoil but determined to turn the assignment in the next day after I looked it over one more time. About one year later, as I was cleaning out my desk, I found the assignment in my top drawer. It dawned on me that I never turned it in and that no one, but no one, had ever even asked about it. All my worrying had been in vain.

Because we do not know who we are—that is, spiritual beings who are already perfect manifestations of the life essence—most of us suffer from some degree of perfectionism with regard to the material world. The desire to be perfect can be a great motivator, but most of the time it simply makes us more conscious of the fact that we are *not* perfect. When things don't go our way and we are unable to make a flawless showing, we often resort to the powerful emotion of anger. Anger is all about our fear of not being in control. It is the result of thinking that we must do everything on our own, that there is no one who can help us. While anger, rage, extreme hostility, indignation, and exasperation are emotions we think can counteract a negative situation, they usually end up making the situation much worse. When we express anger, we not only become hostage to the emotion, we make those around us hostages, too. Angry people are often self-righteous know-it-alls who express displeasure at the slightest disappointment. There is such a thing as justifiable anger, but most of us wouldn't recognize it if we fell over it. Our desire to get ahead and stay ahead at all costs can only result in anger, and anger can only lead to failure.

Anger leads to another powerful, negative emotional state: criticism. Our fear that we are not living up to our own potential, that we are not perfect, that all of our needs are not being satisfied, leads to dissecting others as a way to make ourselves feel better. If we are not perfect, then no one else is either. Every hour of every day we spend a significant amount of time criticizing, judging, and critiquing those around us, from what they are wearing, to how they raise their children, to how they do their job. Disconnected as we are from the knowledge that we and our sisters and brothers are really one, we go out of our way to prove to anyone who will listen that we know how the universe should be run: our way.

Even those people who apparently do not engage in judging and dissecting the lives of others express this destructive tendency through self-criticism. There is a difference between taking an honest inventory of your strengths and weaknesses and ripping yourself to shreds. The self-flagellation process never leads to a positive outcome. It usually results in anger, whether the emotion is expressed outwardly or inwardly. Those who viciously attack themselves are frequently depressed, do not value themselves very highly, and do not feel that they have sufficient power to satisfy their own needs. They are often super-sensitive to their external environment and have a difficult time letting things roll off their backs.

While most of us suffer from jealousy, few of us will admit it. This emotion results from the fear that we will not receive adequate attention for our efforts and that we will lose what we have fought so hard to gain. In our quest for material success, we see others as our enemies. We question and are envious and resentful of the "lucky" breaks and advantages that other people have had. This perspective is victimhood at its finest. Instead of finding out the process that others may have used to realize their dreams, we can only see ourselves as less worthy because we are still struggling to move ahead and succeed. Jealousy is not viewed unfavorably in our culture and is looked at as a "natural" human emotion, whether on the job or in the workplace. But from the vantage point of the Soul, it is very "unnatural" because it is based on fear, separates us from others, and can lead to anger, criticism, and hatred.

Hatred is the most violent and destructive of the emotions and is the result of intense internal fear projected outward. We hate, are violently hostile, or express animosity toward people or circumstances because we believe that we are powerless. Racism is a perfect example of hatred turned against entire peoples simply because they look different from ourselves. We so fear the unknown that it is difficult for us as individuals and as a culture to accept anything or anyone that makes us confront our own lack of adaptability and our own pervading fear of life itself. The interesting thing about hate is that when we confront the person or circumstance in an objective manner, it disappears, and we wonder why we ever felt so intensely in the first place. We still might not completely enjoy the other person or the set of circumstances, but we realize that "different" or "difficult" does not necessarily mean wrong. Hate circumvents our ability to effect positive change in all aspects of our lives, including on the job.

We have seen how the mind, having been conditioned by the events and experiences of the past, has become the absolute ruler in the kingdom of fear. Fear and existential dread are not our birthright as human beings. Rather, they are a response to life based on a gross misinterpretation of the nature of reality. Fear, greed, selfishness, worry, anger, criticism, jealousy, and hatred are not the gifts of self-awareness; rather, they are the obstacles we must overcome in order to recognize our spiritual nature. And the doorway to our spiritual nature is the Soul.

Just as the mind evolves from simple brain functioning to become the seat of our self-conscious awareness, the Soul evolves from the mind when reason develops into higher consciousness. Our Soul, which links us back with our source—energy, God, or Spirit—is not limited by the constraints of time and space and has the wisdom of eternity within its grasp.

The reasoning mind questions why, if innate intelligence guides the animals in their daily lives as well as the infant as it develops into a child, would it abandon us as we evolve into self-conscious beings? Is it logical that the vast ocean of life from whence we came and with which we were completely fused as babies would simply disappear when we begin to think? Is it reasonable to assume that just because this mysterious guiding force cannot as yet be empirically analyzed and catalogued that it does not exist? No, it is neither logical nor reasonable to assume with such self-satisfied pride that the source of all creation does not exist simply because we cannot see it with the naked eye.

Spirit is at work every moment of every day because it is life itself. Mysterious? Yes. Inaccessible? No, because it is all that really exists and it is who we are. In reality, Spirit does not care whether or not we recognize its existence. It does not judge us just because we are blind to its power. It moves forward second after second creating the circumstances of our lives based on what we ask it to give to us. What we *believe* to be true about ourselves and our reality determines what Spirit brings to us.

Did you ever wonder why those people who are ostensibly "lucky" seem to see the good in any situation and do not appear to be afraid of life, but rather embrace it? Most of us say that we want good things—money, success, loving relationships, a good job—but due to our fear, we spend all of our emotional energy complaining, whining, and criticizing everything that we consider negative or bad.

As human beings, we are the most highly developed of all species on earth and have a choice about how we respond to the outside world. In our daily struggle to protect ourselves against evil, however, we perpetrate it by denying the power of good. The Soul is the rational mind that aligns itself with the power of the positive and makes a conscious choice to think, talk, and do good.

A person who is determined to align him or herself to the good naturally responds to life with a totally different set of emotions than the person who is, consciously or not, aligned with bad. Soulful people express faith, kindness, hope, patience, compassion, duty, and love.

Faith results from the belief that we are all living Souls who are connected to one another through Spirit and that each one of us is simply an individual manifestation of this life essence. The underlying assumption behind faith is that the universe is inherently good and that "all is well." The kind of faith we are talking about is not faith in a particular god. It is faith in the process of life itself. Faith means having the courage to go with, not against, the flow of life.

People who express faith are not filled with fear. When, from time to time, this negative emotion appears within their consciousness, they do not deny it, they simply return their attention to the source of all creation that has nurtured them thus far and move forward regardless of the circumstances. No great idea has ever been achieved without the power of faith behind it. Faith is an impenetrable energy field that can move mountains and make dreams become realities. Faith is the precondition of knowledge. If we never allow ourselves to feel faith, we will never have the chance to see its powerful effects. Once we make the decision to align ourselves with this mighty force and our desires manifest in material reality, however, we have the knowledge that the process works.

When we have faith, we are no longer victims of fear. When we are connected to Spirit, the energy of life, we feel its responsiveness to our needs and rejoice at the assistance it provides us. We realize that, contrary to popular belief, we live in an abundant universe. We recognize that our true spiritual birthright, affirmed by Jesus Christ, one of the greatest spiritual leaders of all time, is "Ask and ye shall receive."

When this recognition hits us fully, we are no longer controlled and manipulated by greed and selfishness. Instead, our natural response to others, ourselves, and the world in general is kindness, endless mercy, charity, and generosity. When the Buddha, a king by birth, realized that the material world was full of pain and suffering, he did not curse humanity, return to his palace, shut himself off, and refuse to do anything about it. He responded to the lessons he had learned by going back out into the world to preach his noble eightfold path whose goal was to enable humanity to reach Nirvana, to release itself from the cycle of endless misery. He taught that it was the individual who was responsible for his or her own suffering and that a life of charity and compassion was the road to enlightenment.

Those who are traveling the path to enlightenment are nurtured by one of the most beautiful of all emotions: hope. We have become a culture of people who expect the worst and then are not disappointed when bad things happen. What if we expected the best? Would we be happy when good things happen, or would our fear deceive us into thinking that such occurrences are only coincidental and that we would be punished for having such lofty expectations? We have all experienced the negative results of worry: endless anxiety, the inability to meet life head-on, stomach pain, ulcers, headaches, depression. How many of us allow ourselves to bask in the glow of hope? How many of us have the courage to look for and believe in the good wherever we go? When we foster a perspective that affirms that everything will turn out for the best, even when circumstances look negative, we dignify ourselves by showing understanding of the life process, and we move one step further to uniting with Spirit.

When we are filled with faith, kindness, and hope, the emotion of anger becomes dormant, and patience takes its place. I, for one, have always struggled to be patient, but I never guessed that the reason patience was so difficult for me to express was that I was so full of anger. Most of my emotional energy was spent in various states of unease regarding the circumstances in my life. I wanted gratification, and I wanted it in the present moment. Luckily, as I said earlier, Spirit does not judge, it merely responds, and in the process sometimes provides us with a valuable lesson the implications of which are impossible to escape.

Five years ago, I collaborated with a dear friend of mine on what we believed was a brilliant book proposal. I was unemployed at the time, having quit a most horrible job. I was full of fear, because even though I was determined to begin a new career as a writer, I didn't have enough money to carry me through the process. I had a lot of desire, but not a lot of patience or hope. I cried, screamed, and cursed my circumstances day after day. Needless to say, we didn't write the book.

Shortly after the project fell through, a friend called to tell me that the law firm where I had worked six years before needed someone to coordinate several ongoing cases for a major client. I was relieved and humiliated at the same time. How could I go back to the place where I had worked right out of college? How could I take a job that was less prestigious than the one that I had left years before? How was I going to work for someone whom I was instrumental in promoting? To add insult to injury, I even had to fight to get the job! My ego was devastated, but my funds were depleted. I cursed the heavens, but I bit the bullet and went back.

For three years I struggled to remain calm and patient and to handle my circumstances with the dignity of a spiritual being. Some days I was successful and some days I failed, but I was determined to learn this most difficult lesson. In the end, I was promoted to the position of marketing coordinator, which entailed mostly writing and research. One year later, much more confident of my writing ability thanks to the seemingly negative opportunity placed in my path by Spirit, I quit and began work on this book.

When we are not living by the clock, when we are not enslaved by some irrational time schedule that we have set for our success, life becomes easier, and we are better able to accept what comes our way. Sometimes what we consider detours are really rerouting opportunities to put us into contact with the people we need to pursue our dreams, or the circumstances we need to confront in order to move ahead. When we have faith, hope, and patience, our lives become more relaxed, and we are more easily able to stop criticizing and judging every single thing that happens, every unpleasant person we meet on the path, and every mistake we make on our journey to understand life's mysteries. We are able to show compassion because we know that somehow all of our needs will be met. When you really think about it, it is those people with whom we have difficulty, those trying circumstances, and those mistakes we make that teach us how to become better people. When we show compassion, we are lifted to a higher plane of existence and begin to understand the meaning of what we all struggle so hard to find: unconditional love.

Where there is compassion, there is no room for jealousy. The advantages of other people are the same advantages that we are capable of receiving. The people who are successful are not our enemies; they are our teachers because they remind us what is possible. We are all actors on the stage of life. If we are not happy with the part we are playing, it is our job to rewrite the script. As spiritual beings, as living Souls, we understand that we have a duty to life to put something back.

Duty, which means taking personal responsibility for the circumstances in our lives and fulfilling our spiritual mission, can be a hard pill to swallow because sometimes we are at a loss to understand how we got where we are. When we open up to the Spirit within, we see that we are where we are supposed to be, that there are no "accidents," and that the life energy has our best interests at heart. We need not judge where we work or whom we work with; we need only determine the direction we want to go in, move forward every day, and do whatever is required of us to the absolute best of our ability. Our Soul, in conjunction with Spirit, will take care of the rest.

We have finally come to the most powerful of all the emotions of the Soul: love. Songs extol its virtues, religions preach its power, and yet many of us only love when we know that we'll get something out of it, and even then we don't give it freely, but see it as something that can be given or taken away. It is clear that for many people love does not make the world go round. Selfishness and fear disguised as love do so. "If you love me, I'll love you." "I'll love you even more if you . . ." In actuality, "Spirit", "energy," or "God" are really synonyms for this emotion because the life essence lovingly and generously provides us with all the tools we need to live our life on a material and spiritual level. This love is unconditional because it doesn't judge us if we choose a negative path. It gives us more negativity because that is what we have asked for by focusing all of our energy on it. If we change our course in the direction of the positive, it lovingly changes course right alongside us, no questions asked.

While most people do not deny the power of love, few have the courage to feel it and use it. We talk a good game, but we don't live it. We are afraid to show unselfish, generous affection and warmth toward all living creatures. It's too hard to stand apart from our friends, colleagues, and loved ones by refusing to submit to negative emotion. The sad truth is that until we try to see the positive and focus all of our energy on it by living it, we will never witness the miracles that can be achieved once we are free from the domination of the negative. Spirit, in its infinite wisdom, however, does not care if we feel the power of love or not. It loves because it cannot do anything else. True, unconditional love is not only the antithesis of hate; it has the power of the universe behind it.

When we not only recognize our Soul, but live in conjunction with it, we are inextricably connected to Spirit and we are the masters of our destinies. The first goal on this road to discovering our true identity is to achieve the ability to transmute energy, that is, to transform at will any negative mental emotion into a positive spiritual emotion. As we become more proficient in transmuting energy, we discover that Spirit works according to certain laws, knowledge of which is invaluable to the Soul as it proceeds in the school of life.

Let us go back to science for a moment. Science tells us that (1) everything is made up of energy; (2) energy is synonymous with consciousness; and (3) energy can be neither created nor destroyed. It can only move and change. Theology tells us that God or Spirit is all present, powerful, and knowing. Since we have already concluded that this energy science speaks of is synonymous with Spirit, it is obvious that both schools of thought are saying the same thing. If every living and nonliving thing is nothing but ever-changing, pure energy, and this energy is omnipresent, omnipowerful, and omniscient, then in the most fundamental of respects there are no people, places, situations, or things. There is only energy/Spirit/God.

This being the case, it is logical that, even though we believe— in the workplace and everywhere else—that we are dealing with other people, we are really only dealing, in any situation, with this life essence. While at first glance this appears to be only a fascinating theoretical perspective, it is actually the most liberating of concepts. Since each and every one of us is made up of the exact same thing, we and everyone else, behind the personality, behind the physical appearance, behind the life experience, are identical, even though our individual expressions of this essence are unique.

This idea is the basis of many spiritual systems and is known as the "One Life Principle." This principle, when fully understood, has the power to set us free from the concerns of everyday reality. When we live our lives based on the One Life Principle, rather than in the illusion of many lives, we can no longer judge, criticize, or condemn, because in so doing we are condemning ourselves and life itself. When we are confronted with a greedy, selfish, unkind person who makes our lives miserable, we must step back, recognize that we have attracted this situation to us for some reason, and have the courage to look to our Soul or higher consciousness for guidance. Have you ever noticed that people most often complain about the people who are most like them? It is a painful process to be constantly shown the darkest secrets of our deepest selves through the mirror of other people. But it is more painful if we do not do anything about it.

Everyone, it seems, knows about the law of karma, but many assume that it is the mysterious and esoteric law that governs the reincarnation process. While this may indeed be the case, the law of karma is really the principle of cause and effect, which governs the creation process and operates every second of every day. In order to comprehend the law of karma, we need only understand that the effect is the same as the cause, or put more simply, "As you sow, so shall you reap." Therefore, if you want good things, focus your thoughts on the positive and go about doing good. If you want bad things, focus your thoughts on the negative and go about doing evil. Just like Aladdin's genie, Spirit in all its mercy and love tells those of us who have ears to hear, "Your wish is my command."

The creation process can be likened to the process of birth. Just as the sperm fertilizes the egg which develops into a baby who is ultimately born into material reality, the Soul informs Spirit of its desire through the mediums of thought and action, and eventually the desired outcome materializes in the external world of matter. Just as in the development of a baby, however, there is always an incubation period required after conception and before birth.

When we decide we want to change our lives for the better, we have to be prepared to allow time for the new information to incubate and develop before we can expect a change in our external reality. When we first begin the process of self-change, the incubation period can seem long and arduous. We may be tempted to give up and resort to our old ways. This is the time when we must rely on faith to see us through the difficult passage and keep our negative thoughts and our doubts in check. Eventually, however, if we persist, we will succeed, and then faith in the process of creation will become knowledge of the ultimate truth—that we are truly co-creators. Once we have this knowledge, we become more adept at the process and our actions are more easily inspired by the positive emotion of our Souls. As a result, the incubation period becomes shorter and shorter, until finally our minds become forever joined with our Souls and we are living agents of Spirit.

When we accept our role as co-creators with God or Spirit, life is not as complicated as it seemed previously. Here are a few more spiritual truths that can make a Soul's life more rewarding, joyful, and peaceful:

➤ All needs are fulfilled, so be clear about what needs you establish for yourself. If you want success—think, talk, and act successful, even if your mind resists you every step of the way.

➤ Life is the interplay of opposites, good and bad, light and dark, night and day. If you want good things, do not concern yourself with the bad; look for the positive things in life and make yourself a living example of good.

➤ You attract what you fear the most. Aspire to confront your fears head on with faith, and the secrets of the universe will unfold before you.

➤ Life is cyclical and rhythmic. What goes up must come down. Make the most of the good times and do not be discouraged when the pendulum of life swings the other way. Make the most of your "down" time; use it to assess and correct the beliefs that are holding you back; keep your vision clear; and sow the seeds that you want to harvest when times change for the better.

➤ Stand alone. Do not be influenced by what is going on around you. Everyone is doing the best they can based on the knowledge they have.

➤ Do not concern yourself with other people's affairs. Everything is relative; what is good for you might be bad for someone else.

➤ Don't take this world personally. Spirit's intention is not to make you unhappy; rather it wants you to learn from your mistakes and embrace your highest spiritual nature.

➤ The point of power is in the present moment. The past is over and cannot be undone, and the future is determined by our thoughts and actions in the present.

➤ Work is the creative outlet of the Soul.

The map is not the territory. That is to say, it is not enough to accept a new philosophy of life simply on an intellectual level. As the old saying goes, "Actions speak louder than words." If we want to make positive changes in our lives, we can't just sit on the couch every other day and devote a few moments to thinking positive thoughts. We must totally change the way we think, not because someone tells us that it is the right thing to do, but because we want to live a happy life. It is impossible to live a happy, successful life if we are filled with fear, greed, worry, anger, criticism, jealousy, and hatred.

We must defy our mind's fear-based reality and turn to our Soul, the most highly evolved aspect of ourselves, which has waited patiently for us to ask for help. We must courageously venture into this unknown territory inspired by the example of those who have gone before us. We must begin not only to think positively, but also to act as agents of the ultimate good motivated by faith, kindness, patience, compassion, duty, and love. This is the true meaning of Your Life's Work, on or off the job.

PART TWO

PERSPECTIVE IS EVERYTHING

Once I think I am awake
it becomes so clear
Oh, the dream is deep!

—MICHAEL
MANNION

TWO

LOVING THE WORK YOU DO

We have become a society that desires immediate gratification above all else. More often than not, when we watch television or go to the movies, we see this desire projected onto characters who usually have no real means of earning a living, but who possess everything we want: money, lovely homes, fashionable clothes, flashy cars, and fulfilling relationships. In fact, the shows that portray life "as it is," that is, people who go to work every day, struggle to live decent lives, feed their families, and put their children through school, do not usually last more than one season, or they end up on public television. When we turn off the TV or the VCR, we realize that what we want we don't have, and we become intensely dissatisfied with our own lives which do not even come close to the Madison Avenue or Hollywood version of reality. We see ourselves as failures and we vow to get what we want, even if the price we must pay is unhappiness.

The Buddha didn't need television to recognize that desire is the cause of all human misery. In the modern world, where most of us must go to work every day in order to pay the rent, the result of unsatisfied desire is intimately connected to our jobs, which have become symbols for everything that is wrong with our lives. This resentment leads to self-criticism, worry, boredom, and the imposter or "I'm not worthy" syndrome.

On the spiritual level, however, the real issue behind our dissatisfaction with our jobs, behind our never-ending desire for beautiful homes, designer clothes, and money in the bank is our thwarted desire for happiness and our inability to unite with the creative force of life. We need not make a deal with the devil, trading in our self-worth for success. The law of karma dictates that the cause is the same as the effect. As spiritual beings, if we want happiness, we must be happy now. If we want to find a job that we love, we must love the work that we are doing now.

Let's check in on someone who, despite very trying circumstances, was able to make a leap of faith and learned to love her job.

Kate, age thirty-five, returned to her job at a major university hospital as the coordinator of patient education after a four-month hiatus, during which time she underwent chemotherapy and radiation therapy for cancer. She was successful in healing herself from cancer through the use of alternative methods of healing, including intensive meditation and visualization, in addition to traditional Western medical treatment.

"Before I was diagnosed with cancer, I had conflicting feelings about my job and didn't find it very satisfying. I found my work rather boring and somewhat beneath me. At the same time, I was very critical of myself, worried constantly that I wasn't up to the job and had problems delegating and prioritizing work. The bottom line was clear: I didn't find much meaning in my job. While I was recovering from the cancer, I realized that part of my continued healing had to include a change in my attitude about my career. I also realized that through fighting the cancer, I had developed the tools and the inner power necessary to make my job rewarding and meaningful.

"It seems simple, but when I returned to the office, I made sure that I took care of my Soul's needs, as well as my job responsibilities. I took a lunch break every day, as well as a morning and an afternoon break to meditate and collect my thoughts. Every few hours I would check in with myself to see how I was reacting to my environment and, if necessary, to make 'attitude adjustments.' I also kept an ongoing list of the positive aspects of my job and of the things I was doing well, as well as the impact these things had on my coworkers and on the patients in the hospital. Amazingly, I started liking my job. I know now that my illness helped me to realize that I wake up every morning to live, not simply to go to work. I am currently exploring other possible career paths that may ultimately be more suitable to my goals and desires, but I now believe that any work I do is a creative expression of myself. It is quite liberating to know that every day is an opportunity to grow, and that there is meaning in everything."

Kate's inspirational story goes to the heart of the issue surrounding how to go about loving your job, but it is much more than that. I am honored that this woman is my friend and so willingly shared her intimate journey with me. I vividly remember the day that she called me to tell me that she had been diagnosed with cancer. When the phone rang, I was sitting at work, suffering from a bad attitude and struggling with getting a press release finished on time. Her calm, peaceful demeanor immediately melted my usual overactive intensity on the job. I forgot about the press release and was immediately transported to a better place.

After she made sure that I was doing well, she told me that

the doctors had found a very large tumor in her chest and that she had been diagnosed with lymphoma. I was distraught, but determined to be strong and supportive. I noticed that even though she had just been diagnosed with the disease, she talked about the cancer in the past tense—as if she had already been healed. I have never been more in awe of another person in my entire life. I know that I would have been hysterical and totally unable to have such faith in a successful result, so soon after being told that I had a life-threatening illness.

Kate's doctors were all amazed at how fast she healed. But what they didn't know was that Kate never for a moment considered herself to be sick. The tumor went away because Kate saw the illness for what it was: a call to action on the spiritual level. Needless to say, this woman is an amazing human being. I only hope that I, and all of us, can reach her level of understanding and love.

CRISIS AS AN OPPORTUNITY FOR SPIRITUAL AWAKENING

Just as Kate used her illness as a springboard for further spiritual development, we can use any crisis—even the crisis of job dissatisfaction—the same way.

Everyone who has ever worked anywhere has intimate knowledge of job dissatisfaction. I remember how struck I was when the recognition first hit me that 99.9 percent of the people with whom I worked in my first years in a law firm, from messengers up to senior partners, seemed to hate their jobs. It didn't dawn on me then that the reason I could only see the people who hated their jobs was that I myself hated my job.

One of the most important and difficult of all the spiritual truths is that we see the world only as a reflection of how we see ourselves. This was proven to me by the fact that when I returned to the firm after several years, during which time I had been seeing a psychotherapist and studying spirituality, I was amazed by the fact that more people seemed to be enjoying their work. Just as I realized that I must be feeling better about my work life if I could even recognize these happy people, I was firmly reminded that I hadn't gone far enough because I was not yet as happy as I wanted to be.

Every day for four years, I ran into the same messenger. Every day when I asked him how he was doing, he responded with the biggest smile I had ever seen in my entire life, "Great. Never been better. Do you need anything delivered?" At first this guy used to really annoy me. He was *never* upset. He would laugh if he got caught in the rain delivering a package. He would smile whenever things got tough. He really got on my nerves.

I have always been cynical by nature and I was skeptical that anyone who earned little more than minimum wage and probably had to live with his parents in order to make ends meet could have such a cheerful attitude. But, little by little, I began to look forward to seeing him because on a deep level he made me feel good. As my natural cynical nature became less and less useful in my quest for spiritual fulfillment, I began to emulate him. And, like magic, I always ran into him when I was harassed, harried, or ready to scream. I now realize that this messenger was really Spirit's messenger sent to show me and anyone else caught up in the crisis of job dissatisfaction the meaning of duty and love. I realized that he had changed my life when the partner who sat in the office next to mine stopped me in the hall one day right before I resigned to fulfill my dream of becoming a writer and said, "Does anything bother you? Have you always been this cheerful? How did you get such a great attitude?" As I was about to respond, I noticed my favorite messenger standing further down the hallway, smiling at me.

RAMIFICATIONS OF A MENTAL APPROACH TO LIFE AND WORK

Job dissatisfaction, just like a disease, affects our lives in the most negative of ways and calls into question the very meaning of life itself. When we spend more time groaning about our work and dodging our responsibilities than we do actually working, we affirm the negative and deny the power of Spirit.

When we say that our jobs lack meaning, what we are really saying is that our lives lack meaning. This is a very dangerous predicament to be in. Where there is no meaning, there is no understanding of the creative process of life, no hope, only fear and despair. Just as flowers cannot bloom where there is no water, life cannot bloom where there is no love and faith.

Kate discovered that the only solution to her existential quest for survival and meaning was through the doorway of the Soul. But she didn't stop there. She walked through the door. If we want to find meaning and answers, we must relinquish the hold that our minds have on us. We cannot serve two masters, the material and the spiritual, at the same time. Our minds are our link to material reality but they are flawed, they cannot move beyond the experiences of the past. They cannot anticipate a bright future because they are stuck in the despair and longing of our desire. The mind is a beautiful but outmoded instrument that serves to keep us alive by alerting us to all the danger in the world, while at the same time keeping us from taking risks and moving ahead by holding us hostage to a life of endless reruns of past failures.

When we are governed by the failures of the past, we are plagued by fear, self-criticism, boredom, and worry. Nothing is very interesting. No assignment or project on the job can hold our attention for very long. We are so lacking in energy that it is an effort to even get up in the morning. We worry, feeling as bad as we do, how we are going to manage to do enough work to slide by, get our paycheck, and pay our bills. Our anger at the lack of meaning in our lives, which once turned outward, begins to turn inward. We become depressed, even if we don't know it, and start to see ourselves as imposters who are not worthy of a better job, a better life. Our work suffers even more. We can't seem to prioritize our assignments. We are incapable of delegating. We feel as if we have to do everything by ourselves. We are afraid to ask for help. We feel trapped. I've been there, you've been there, we've all been there. It's not a pretty picture.

It is our Souls, connected to the eternity and the infinity of Spirit, that can heal us and lift us out of this swamp of devastating self-annihilation. Only our Souls lead us to achieve our highest dreams and aspirations. But the only way to the Soul is to surrender our lives to Spirit.

THE TRUE MEANING OF HEALING

To heal means to make right. When something goes terribly wrong on any level—physical, mental, or spiritual—the first thing a person needs is proper perspective. When Kate discovered that she had cancer, she put it in its proper perspective by recognizing that the illness was not simply a disease of her body, but also a disease of her Soul. There is a connection between not finding meaning in everyday reality and in getting sick. She didn't shrink from this realization. She forged ahead and took care of business—her body's business and her Soul's business. She used all resources at her disposal, including traditional Western medical treatment and alternative forms of healing, both of which had a significant impact on her rapid recovery, and on her later ability to transform her job.

When faced with the cancer of job dissatisfaction, the same exact method applies. Once we can honestly diagnose the true nature of our condition, we can see it in its proper perspective and begin to heal ourselves by uncovering the reasons for its existence. Sometimes the most imortant reason is that we have sold ourselves short and have settled for a job that is less challenging than we are prepared to handle or is not in keeping with our personality structure. Anger at our lack of courage to pursue what we really want or to find a job that nurtures us results in misery. There are times when a radical change in our work lives is required in order to find out why we are dissatisfied.

A well-educated acquaintance of mine, whom I shall call Joe, landed a terrific, well-paying job right out of college, in the regional development office of a major university. He was smart, had well-developed interpersonal skills, and was a self-motivated person. For the first six months, Joe shared the office with his dynamic, likable boss, and his job progressed nicely. Things started to fall apart when his boss left for a new job, leaving him to run the office alone. Due to financial constraints, the university decided that his boss would not be replaced. Joe tried to rise to the occasion but found that he could not. He suffered from intense loneliness, became depressed, and began to hate his job. In addition, he felt like a failure because he realized that he could no longer motivate himself even when his work was challenging.

Despite urging from friends and family to stick with it because he was making such a good salary, Joe decided to quit without another job. He was single, hadn't yet accumulated any debt, and felt that he had nothing to lose except his sanity. He went on a lot of interviews, but nothing struck him as appropriate or interesting. The money he had put away soon ran out, and he was forced to find a job in order to make money. To the horror of many people in his life, he took a job as a messenger with an advertising company.

When I asked him how the job was going, he told me that he really liked it because it gave him a lot of time to think about his possibilities for the future. He further explained that he now realized that he had been miserable in his former job because he needed the company of other people to energize him. Joe loved to bounce ideas off other people and responded well in a team situation. He told me that his loneliness had been the cause of all his misery. In retrospect, I am amazed at Joe's courage and at the understanding he developed about what he needed in order to be happy on the job. As a messenger, he had time to reflect on his circumstances, and this led to healing.

After six months as a messenger, the company asked him to take a position in their accounting department. He accepted and found that while he was very good at accounting, he didn't much like the work because, once again, he didn't get to interact very often with other people. As a result of his experiment in the accounting department, Joe was even more determined to find a people-oriented job.

One day, out of the blue, an old friend invited Joe out to lunch to tell him about his new job in public relations. After hearing about his friend's job, Joe knew what he wanted to do. His friend volunteered to help him get in the door at his company, and Joe graciously accepted the assistance. He is now a highly respected executive in a public relations firm.

Sometimes, however, the urge to leap into a new career leads to desperation and bad decisions. I should know. After three and a half years as the coordinator of litigation legal assistants in a law firm, I decided that I couldn't take it anymore. I had originally gone to work in the legal field because I thought that I wanted to become a lawyer. After I decided that I didn't, I stayed on and was promoted to a management role.

On one particularly horrible day, while I was sitting in my office with my head in my hands praying for a new job, the phone rang. It was the owner of an executive recruitment agency who had somehow received a copy of my résumé. She asked if I would be interested in transferring my skills to the field of executive recruitment. I jumped at the chance. The interviews went well, and I took the job, more in an attempt to escape my job dissatisfaction than in an effort to make a career change. Because I hadn't dealt with why I felt such intense job dissatisfaction at my former job, I found myself facing even greater job dissatisfaction in my new job. Not only that, but I was worse off financially because my fear held me back from doing a good job. It took everything I had in me not to quit, but something within me told me to keep at it until I figured out why this situation had occurred.

I now realize that, in the midst of my emotional and physical pain (I developed sciatica as a result of not having been able to "stand the job"), I was given no choice but to surrender to Spirit, which thankfully saved me from a complete nervous breakdown. After about six months, I became pretty good at finding people jobs, and due to my own experience fleeing my former job without self-knowledge, I became adept at uncovering what my applicants' true motivations were in wanting new jobs. More surprisingly, despite my negative environment, I found that I was enjoying what I was doing. Even though I was now making good money, I left this job after a year, this time for a job that I truly loved.

Despite my happy ending after several painful years running from my own role in creating the conditions of my work life, it is necessary to face the fact that many of us are no longer recent high school or college graduates and do not have the luxury of learning these lessons on a hit-or-miss basis. It might seem easier to begin fresh somewhere else, but oftentimes there are circumstances beyond our control, such as mortgage payments, the need for a second income, or the demands of single parenthood that make it necessary for us to stick with the job we have. In reality, even if you can afford the luxury of quitting, it is often much better and more practical to confront your situation head-on where you are than to land in the same situation somewhere else the way I did.

What separates the people who find joy in performing seemingly meaningless tasks like delivering packages from the people who cannot find joy even in challenging work? The obvious answer is that those who find joy understand that no task performed in service to Spirit is a meaningless task. These individuals, and I have met many, have surrendered their lives to a force greater than themselves. As a result, they are able to keep their vision firmly in mind at all times and are not easily distracted by negative influences. They are in the world but not of it. They know that their self-worth is not determined by the work they do, but rather by how they do their work.

"SEEK FIRST THE SPIRITUAL THINGS AND ALL ELSE SHALL BE ADDED UNTO YOU"

Recognition of the reasons for our dissatisfaction leads nowhere if it is not followed by action. Let's return to Kate's story for a moment. After she successfully healed herself from cancer, she was determined to heal her attitude about her job. She turned her life over to her own inner power, her Soul, and she made seemingly minor but powerful changes in her daily routine. She took a lunch break every day, as well as a morning and afternoon break to meditate and collect her thoughts. Even though taking breaks from our work doesn't seem like much, it is. I used to be so stressed on the job and so intense about getting my work done that I considered those who had time to take lunch or to collect their thoughts wimps. How wrong I was. I was the wimp because

I put greater emphasis on my desire for material success than on my spiritual needs.

Even though our society is now in the midst of a great transformation, we still value material perfection above spiritual evolution. Our individual worth is measured by how much stress and pain we can take, not by how much love and joy we are able to feel. We prefer the fast track to the meaningful track. We are so caught up in getting more and achieving more that we have lost touch with the things that really matter. This is more than sad, it is pathetic. How many people do you know who may be rich and ostensibly powerful, but who cannot even remember what day of the year their children were born?

Our self-righteous indignation toward those who live happy, contented lives is really the result of cowardice. We believe that it is better to be rich and in control than to be happy and loved. We prefer desire to aspiration and material comfort to inner peace. As a people, we may be invincible in the face of foreign attack, but we lack true courage because we refuse to align ourselves with the only power there is: Spirit. Is it any wonder that most of us are miserable?

We can't satisfy our needs on the job, or in any aspect of life, because we can't relax. When we can't relax, we cannot contact our Souls. When we can't contact our Souls, we are dominated by the negative emotions of the mind. We can't see the situations we face with any degree of objectivity, much less make a plan of action that will work. Let us not stick our noses in the air like I did, judging those individuals who have the courage to enjoy their lives. All of us have the same ability that Kate has. All of us can take a few moments out of our busy day to treat ourselves with the respect worthy of spiritual beings.

THE POWER OF THE POSITIVE

When we relax and allow ourselves to contact our higher consciousness, remarkable things happen. Miraculously, things don't look quite as bad as they did a moment before. We can step back, get in touch with what we are feeling, and as Kate says, make "attitude adjustments." Sitting comfortably, we can visualize what we want to happen. We can transmute our negative emotional energy into positive, life-affirming energy. When we become filled with the peace of eternity, and feel the unconditional love of Spirit, we can go back out into the external world and do whatever we have to do with compassion, hope, and faith leading the way.

One way to keep yourself firmly planted in the sea of positive energy is to keep a list of the positive aspects of your job and your accomplishments, as well as a running record of how you have positively affected your coworkers and your work environment. This is not a Pollyanna solution to a serious problem. It is an affirmation of what is good about not only your job, but also yourself. Reading or thinking about the good changes the kind of energy that flows through your body, and you are better able to meet the demands made on you. When you focus on the positive, recognizing that the power that is motivating you is the same power that created the entire universe, you are truly acting as a co-creator with Spirit.

As I said, I am cynical and skeptical by nature. Luckily, however, I do not have endless tolerance for pain and suffering. I, like most everyone else, do not like feeling bad for extended periods of time. If given a preference, I will choose joy over pain, and that is why I began to delve into spirituality.

When I learned the simple truth that all I needed to do in times of stress was to relax and redirect my thoughts from the negative to the positive, I was thrilled. One day at work, however, my ability to put my new knowledge into practice was severely tested. Everything that could have gone wrong went wrong. Everyone was in a bad mood. My computer broke. I got caught in the rain at lunchtime, and my hair looked like a mop. I spilled coffee all over some important papers on my desk. A friend called to say that her grandfather had died. I was not feeling connected to anything except the absurd misery of life. I closed my office door and began to cry. I wanted to give up and go home. I admitted defeat. I was broken. I had no choice. I asked my Soul for help.

I stopped crying just as the Beatles song "All You Need is Love" started going through my head. I started laughing uproariously as I imagined John Lennon as an angel with wings standing before me. My reverie was cut short, however, when my phone began to ring. The meanest partner in the entire firm was on the other end of the line. Everyone hated this man. He never said anything nice. All he ever did was yell. "Tami," he said, on the verge of screaming, "you did a lousy job on that assignment I gave you! You screwed everything up, and I think you're an idiot." Someone other than me responded, "I'm sorry. I guess I'm not perfect. I'll come up right now, and you can tell me how you'd like me to redo it." I couldn't believe it, but I didn't even feel badly about what he had said. I went up to his office and smiled at him. He was nicer to me than he had ever been before.

Because I was calm, centered within myself, and focused on the positive, the partner's mean words could not find a home in my being. Further, I was able to transmute his negative energy into positive energy simply by responding to him out of faith, not fear. And, unaware that anything miraculous had occurred, he responded in kind.

WORK AS THE CREATIVE EXPRESSION OF THE SOUL

When we can get past the negativity and reconnect with our true nature, we can see work in its true light. Work is not getting up and going to your job day after day. It does not mean struggle and sacrifice. Work is our spiritual duty. To live is to work. Our Souls creatively express themselves in the material world by how we do our work, regardless of whether this work takes the form of delivering packages, raising a child, or planning a city. To Spirit, it is all the same. Let's return to science for a moment. Scientifically speaking, work is defined as nothing more than an exchange of energy. When we give out negative energy, the work we perform is hard labor. When we give out positive energy, we do not work in the traditional sense, we love.

Each and every one of us has suffered too long and too hard by seeing our work and our lives as meaningless. It is not logical that the creative power that made us in its own image would abandon us in a meaningless world. It is not logical that this great force would endow us with the ability to reason and to think inwardly if it didn't intend for us to use our self-awareness to embrace the gift of life.

We can run from our highest selves, our Souls, but we cannot hide. Whether we recognize it or not, we are always evolving. The energy that created us never rests. It never gets tired or bored. It doesn't get frustrated. It simply moves and changes. We can make our evolutionary process much more pleasant. We can even have a good time along the way. All we have to do is reestablish our connection with our Souls, the part of us that is always at one with Spirit, the guardian of our highest dreams and aspirations that already lives within the kingdom of heaven.

THE POINT OF POWER IS IN THE PRESENT

Everything happens in the present. We can recall the events of the past, but we cannot change them. We can envision what might happen in the future, but it is our actions in the present moment that dictate what sort of future we will have. The past and the future are illusions. The only time that exists in any real sense is the present moment. When we dedicate ourselves to living not in the past and not in the future, but one moment at a time, we are free.

When we are not shackled by past mistakes or future concerns, we have more than enough time to devote to living as Souls. When we make even a meager attempt to live in the present, our Souls provide us access to the wisdom of Spirit, and everything seems to make perfect sense, even the bad things. No longer standing on flat terrain and suffering from limited vision, we are lifted to the summit of the mountain and can see forever. We understand that there is no reason to fear because we now know, beyond a shadow of a doubt, that we are Spirit, and that Spirit is eternal.

THREE

COPING WITH LAYOFFS AND
OTHER FAILURES

Sometimes, even when we think we're doing everything right, life throws us a curveball. These days, many, if not most, of us have either been threatened by the possibility of a layoff or have actually found ourselves without a job as a result of downsizing. When we are faced with the inability to meet our financial commitments, it is very difficult to keep a positive outlook and move forward with confidence and hope. Just the hint that our jobs are not secure fills us with fear and existential dread. Perhaps it is at this moment that we are forced to face the extent to which we have defined ourselves and our self-worth by our jobs. The question of how we will be able to pay our rent sends us into a quagmire of anxiety and despair that even the most positive-thinking people among us have difficulty overcoming.

I grew up in Pittsburgh, and in my childhood the city's economy was still dependent on a strong steel-making industry that employed many thousands of people. In the 1970s, however, the steel industry, once the pride of America, was no longer considered viable or competitive in the international arena. My father worked for the steelworkers' union, which is headquartered in Pittsburgh, and our family witnessed how the breakdown of this industry affected the lives of the steelworkers whom my father represented.

It was a sad time. For many steelworkers, making steel was not only a job, it was a family tradition. Generations ago, the steel mill was the only game in town for immigrants of many nationalities who had come to the United States to make a better life for themselves. The journey of these people to transform their status as low-paid immigrant labor into middle-class industrial workers was a hard-fought battle. Just as the goal had been reached, they found themselves dispensable. The fundamental issue for those affected by this unfortunate set of circumstances was not whether or not the dismantling of the steel industry should have happened, but rather that it did happen.

There was no easy answer to the question, If I'm not a steelworker, who am I? Not unsurprisingly, there were many who didn't immediately make the adjustment to the new economic reality; many slipped into despair, believing that it was too late for them to retrain for other jobs. For those families who were broken by these events, it was the next generation who would adapt to the changing times, but not without having first learned the fearful lessons of their elders. Of course, there were many who rebounded and sought retraining or further education with or without help from government agencies. They may have resented their situation, but they did not allow their lives to be broken. They valued themselves too highly. They did not consider themselves merely as steelworkers, but as worthwhile human beings.

Unfortunately, it wasn't only the steel industry that was affected. Most other blue-collar workers have also found their lives permanently changed. While these workers were confronting these painful lessons, many who were better educated and working in more "prestigious" white-collar jobs did not show much compassion, sympathy, or respect for their plight. They did not see that we are all connected through the vast chain of being and that one person's struggle is everyone's struggle. They did not see that the changing economic landscape was about to land right on their doorstep. Now the entire workforce of our country is facing the same situation that the steelworkers and other industrial workers confronted a few decades ago. How will we adapt? Jim's story might give us some direction.

Jim, age fifty, is currently a freelance writer working out of his home office in the Southwest. Prior to his writing career, he was the director of administration in an architectural firm in the Northeast. He lost his job when his firm merged with another firm. When it first became clear that his job was not secure, Jim felt like a failure and remembered his father's difficulty finding work after being laid off as an auto worker in Detroit. He painfully recalled how his dad's life had been crushed by his inability to rebound after this event. Jim couldn't help himself. Faced with the loss of his own job, he was angry and filled with self-righteous indignation. Next, after reality set in, he began to panic about what his next career move should be. In contrast to the situation faced by his father, Jim knew that he could probably find another job in his field and continue to earn a very good salary. But this option didn't appeal to him on a gut level and made him feel even more depressed. After much fearful internal deliberation, worry, and doubt, he decided that his next move should be one that would satisfy his longtime desire to work for himself and to write. After speaking with his wife and children, Jim decided that what the family needed was a complete change in lifestyle.

"We sold our home and rented a house in Arizona, where I could earn a living as a freelance writer and pursue my lifelong dream of writing a novel. At first I was petrified of such a huge change and how my family would react once we had made the move. But I realized that if I was ever going to satisfy my need to create, I would have to take the risk. I could either look at the loss of my previous career as a horrible twist of fate or as an opportunity provided me by the universe to satisfy what my Soul had been urging me to do for the past ten years.

"To be honest, the first year in Arizona was tough. Every hour on the hour I doubted my ability to pursue my dream and worried whether I had made the right decision. Eventually, however, it became clear to me that I was the one setting up obstacles to success and that my wife and kids were very happy because I had finally become an active member of the family. I was shocked when I realized that by meeting my own needs and communicating them to my wife and children, I was also meeting their need to develop a deeper connection with me.

"I started writing articles on administration issues for trade magazines and doing consulting work to make extra money. I also started my novel. When I realized that I was happy for the first time in my life, my anxiety disappeared. Every day I thank the universe for providing me with the opportunity to change my life."

CONFRONTING YOUR SITUATION HEAD-ON

Let's face it, when we are faced with a layoff, we feel like a failure, even if the situation is completely beyond our control. When Jim first realized that he was about to be jobless, his first reaction was a flashback to fear. He couldn't help but remember how his father's life was destroyed after he was laid off. He couldn't help but project the fear that his father felt when faced with such devastating circumstances onto his own life. That's what the mind does. It doesn't mean to be cruel. Because its sense of reality is dominated completely by the past and because it only wants to ensure our self-preservation at all costs, it has no other recourse but to replay the failures and defeats of the past as a way to warn us of danger ahead. When circumstances arise that threaten its survival, it strikes back the only way it knows how: through anger, indignation, and panic.

That's okay—for a while. So get it out of your system. Get mad, be self-righteous, blame everything and everyone for your circumstances. Throw a big fit. Feel sorry for yourself. Cry and scream and curse the economy, the politicians, God, your mother and father, your first-grade teacher. Get a punching bag or engage in some activity that requires that you expend a lot of energy, and release the pain and fear.

One note of caution is in order. Taking your pain out on your spouse, loved ones, and especially your children can only lead to greater pain and misery. When we take out our feelings on children, we sometimes do irreparable harm. It is no great secret that children are very impressionable. They also understand more about what is going on than we give them credit for. By honestly sharing your feelings with them, you can gain greater insight into what is really important.

Children learn to react to life based on how their parents or caregivers react to life. Do you want them to see you as the sort of person who cannot control him or herself? Do you want them to see you as someone who is easily broken? Do you want them to fear life? Or would you prefer that they see you as the sort of person who has great self-control? Wouldn't it be better to teach them how to adapt to the changing circumstances of life with faith, hope, and honesty?

RESPONDING TO FAILURE

After we release our initial feelings of anger, indignation, and panic, we come to a crossroads. We can either see our circumstances as a horrible twist of fate and keep the negativity going, or we can see the situation with which we are faced as an opportunity provided us by the creative power of the universe to move forward and evolve.

When we give complete power to our minds, we have no other alternative but to see ourselves as the puppets of fate, as victims. For many years I was in the job placement and recruitment field. I saw many people come and go, and the main factor that determined who got what job, and in what time frame, was the attitude of the person looking for a job. I must admit that I really enjoyed the hard cases because I am such a perfectionist that I figured that anyone could place the perfect candidates, but who would take care of the rest, if not me? One candidate, though, really pushed me right into the arms of my Soul.

Susan, a secretary who was laid off when her company went through a downsizing, had been unemployed for about six months and was unable to find another job. She was miserable and couldn't understand why she was still jobless. On paper, she had excellent skills. Out of desperation, Susan borrowed money from her parents and decided to seek further education as a solution to her problem. I met her after she graduated from a three-month paralegal training program.

As she sat in my office during our initial interview, I remember thinking that I had never met a more defensive and negative person in all my life. I was so put off by her that I could barely muster up the energy to ask her questions. Her response to any question that I posed began and ended with an attack on some person, place, or situation. The world was against her, and it wasn't her fault.

Despite my personal and vain quest to be the Mother Teresa of the placement field, I was about to admit defeat and tell her that I didn't think I could do much for her, when she began to cry. When I asked her why she was crying, she told me that she was so tired of failing, but she didn't know what to do about it. Something inside me screamed, "Move in for the kill, you idiot!" Against my better intellectual judgment, I got up from my chair, put my arm around her, and told her that she had come to the right place. I would help her find a job if she would open her heart and her mind and be willing to see her life from a new perspective. Sobbing, she agreed.

Susan did not change overnight. Every day for a month she tested my patience by calling to complain, whine, and moan. I listened politely, but with clenched teeth I forced myself to tell her what a great person she was, how courageous she was, and how much she had to offer. Finally she softened up. I had been able to arrange a job interview for her with someone I knew wouldn't kill me if Susan acted like the victim of the century. I told Susan about the interview, but told her that in order to get the job, she would have to make a leap of faith.

I took a risk and asked this most negative of people whom she admired most in the world and why. She thought for a few moments and then responded that it was her deceased grandmother, because despite the fact that she had such a hard life, she was a caring, thoughtful, and loving individual who had always been there for her. I almost fell off my chair! When I regained my composure, I told her to keep the image of her grandmother firmly in her mind as we went over some questions that she might be asked at the interview. Despite a few glitches, Susan responded to the questions with a whole new attitude.

As we concluded our discussion, I could tell that she felt much better about herself. She said, "Do you mean to tell me that all I have to do is act like my grandmother?" Something inside me said, No, act like who you really are. Susan got the job, and I got further into spirituality.

What if we don't need to put obstacles in our path? What if we don't need to go through some long, drawn-out process filled with worry, doubt, and panic to see that every failure is an opportunity in disguise?

HERE COMES THE SUN . . .

The key to spiritual power is to be able to change negative emotion into positive energy at will. Jim struggled with his emotions and found out that the process wasn't easy, due to the deep hold fear had over him. Transmuting energy is not a one-time event, it is an ongoing journey. A recent day in my life proved this to me.

For some reason, I woke up in a bad mood. As I was drinking my first cup of coffee, I was immediately disturbed as the phone rang. It was a good friend who wanted to complain. I not only listened to her complain, I joyfully joined in by complaining about everything and everyone. It felt so good to complain. But halfway through the conversation, a voice inside me asked me why I was being so negative. The sun was out, the apartment was clean, I was having people over for dinner that night and knew that I'd have a good time. What was wrong with me? I changed direction and started talking more positively. So did my friend. I got off the phone feeling like Superwoman.

A few hours later, I went out to buy groceries for my dinner party. As I was walking down the street, I saw someone who lived in my building. I immediately got angry because this man never speaks to me and always acts as if he doesn't see me when we run into each other on the street. I decided to fight fire with fire and to ignore him before he got the chance to ignore me. For about a minute I felt great as I wallowed in my meaningless vengeance. Then it dawned on me. Maybe he would have spoken to me if I hadn't acted like an idiot. Even if he didn't, just what was stopping me from saying hello to him? Maybe he was just shy. I was smiling at my own stupidity, when I ran into another man from my building. This time I went out of my way to say hello. He seemed so happy to see me, and even though we really didn't know each other very well, he gave me a huge smile and said how great I looked. I felt like Superwoman once again.

Three hours later, as my friends were supposed to arrive for dinner, the phone rang. They were going to be an hour late. I hung up the phone really annoyed. I called them every name in the book, after which my boyfriend, who was the one preparing the dinner, asked why I was so irritated since he was the one who should be annoyed and wasn't. I sat down on the couch and relaxed for a moment. So what if my friends were late? It wasn't the end of the world after all. All-out nuclear war was not about to break out. I smiled my Superwoman smile and turned on some music. A few minutes later the buzzer rang. My friends were able to make it to our apartment earlier than they'd expected. We all had a great time, and when I went to bed that night, I was exhausted but happy.

These examples may seem trivial, but they are not. Every day is not a Broadway musical. Some days, every second tests our ability to transmute the negative into the positive, especially when we find ourselves faced with looking for a new job or beginning a new career. It is virtually impossible to act like a Soul every minute of every day, but we must realize that nothing worth having comes without practice. Simply put, those who endure, win.

Maggie, a very dear friend of mine, recently lost her job as a legal recruiter when the law firm where she worked dissolved. Even though she had a few months to get used to the idea, she was depressed and angry when she woke up that first morning with nowhere to go. Like Jim, she knew that while she could most definitely find another job in her field, she didn't really want to keep doing the same old thing. What she wanted was to get out of the law firm environment and get a job in a corporation as a recruiter.

Maggie's desire to switch gears from a legal environment to a corporate environment doesn't seem like such a hard thing to do given the fact that as a legal recruiter, she already had close to ten years of recruiting experience. But in today's overly structured marketplace, it is harder than it seems. "Once a legal recruiter, always a legal recruiter," was the ongoing refrain Maggie heard from the headhunters with whom she was working. There were many people, including Maggie, however, who knew that what she wanted was clearly not beyond the realm of possibility.

She had her good days and her bad days, but she persevered. She came to the conclusion that if the headhunters weren't going to be able to help her, she would just have to help herself. She would have to overcome the doubt placed in her mind by those who seemingly knew more than she did. She didn't do this by repressing her fear or worry; rather, she simply granted herself permission to devote equal time to faith and hope.

As a recruiter and as a person, Maggie had always gone out of her way to help others to find jobs by using her contacts within and outside the legal profession. Even though she found it un-comfortable to network on her own behalf, she pushed past her discomfort and began making calls to everyone she knew, and it paid off. After a few weeks of pursuing her new course of action, she arranged for an informational interview with a recruiter at a major investment firm who was an acquaintance of a friend.

This recruiter took a liking to Maggie and, despite her lack of corporate recruiting experience, arranged an interview for her with the head of corporate recruiting. When she didn't get the job, all of her old doubts and fears returned. But she kept going and through another friend scheduled another interview with the human resources manager of an accounting firm. She didn't get this job either, simply because the position had been temporarily put on hold. She continued to struggle with doubt, anxiety, and worry and began to think that she might as well return to the legal environment. She noticed, however, that even though her faith in her desire to change direction in her career was fading, it had not completely disappeared. She decided to give herself a little more time. Then it happened. The investment firm called to offer her a different position. She took the job.

Within two weeks of her starting work as a corporate recruiter, two of the headhunters who hadn't been able to help her and who doubted that she'd be able to succeed, called her at her new job. It seemed that they now had corporate recruiting positions for which she would be suitable. It's funny how that works, isn't it?

RISK-TAKING AS A CREATIVE, SPIRITUAL PROCESS

Moving back to Jim for a minute, once he got past his anger and moved into a calm place, he could see that there had been something inside of him that had been urging him for a long time to pursue his dream of writing and working for himself. For Jim, the ramifications of his dream meant moving his family from their comfortable surroundings in the Northeast to the less expensive Southwest. Symbolically speaking, in order to pursue his dream, he had to make the decision to become a stranger in a strange land. He had to venture into the unknown territory of the Southwest and the unknown territory of his Soul at the same time.

But before we can take the steps necessary to do what we want to do, we first must recognize that each of us has a dream. From my experience in the recruitment field, I have found that this first step is actually the most difficult. As a rule, we are not encouraged to pursue what has heart and meaning for us. We are encouraged by our parents, our high school and college placement offices, and others who supposedly know what is best for us to get a job and to make money to support ourselves. When we listen to those around us who discourage us from doing what we want to do, we sell ourselves short and we become angry and resentful on a deep level and even begin to deny that we have dreams.

Several years ago, I was helping Meg, a paralegal in her late twenties, find a new job. She was intelligent, had a great résumé, excellent references, and was making a decent salary, but she had been unhappy in all her jobs so far and didn't know why. When I asked Meg what her dream job would be, she looked at me with a blank expression that indicated to me that she had no idea. I then asked her why she had pursued her current occupation, and she responded, "Because I was told that I could make good money."

I thought for a few seconds and then asked her what she had wanted to be when she was a child. After several moments, Meg replied, "I wanted to be an artist, but my parents discouraged me from pursuing art because it didn't pay." I asked her if she already had all the money she needed, would she pursue her dream of becoming an artist? She replied, "Of course, but I can't base my life on a fantasy. I need to make money." It was then that it dawned on me. People do not pursue their dreams because they think they can't. The sad truth is that if you do not give yourself permission to pursue what you want to do, you will never be satisfied with any job.

Of course, in reality making money is a real concern. When we have the courage to imagine what our lives would be like if money were not part of life's equation, however, our dreams move from being trapped in our unconscious minds, where we have kept them under lock and key, to our conscious awareness, where we can figure out if it is possible to achieve them. Our childhood dreams do not go away, because they live within our dormant Souls, which want nothing more than to express themselves in the real world. We have material needs and we have spiritual and creative needs, and both need to be met if we want to be happy.

We can use a layoff or the loss of a job for other reasons to help ourselves to evolve. But we must be honest with ourselves if we want to transform failure into triumph. After we realize that we have dreams, we must ask ourselves whether or not we have the courage to do what it will take to realize them. Are we willing to compromise? Are we willing to do what must be done in order to get where we want to go?

We know from Jim's story that he was willing to make the changes necessary to pursue his goal. After he discussed the situation with his wife and family, they all agreed that the risk was worth taking. Jim didn't just jump right into his new career in one fell swoop, though. He had to figure out a creative way to satisfy both his material needs and his spiritual needs at the same time. He decided to use the expertise he had acquired in his former career to make money by consulting and writing articles on issues on which he was already an expert. Whatever time was left was devoted to beginning his novel. He was scared, but he knew that he was halfway home so he pushed past his fear and continued to move forward.

Just because all of us can't pick up and move our families out of state and begin consulting work doesn't mean that there are not creative solutions to our problems. Let's shift back to Meg to see what the average person with an average job can do to meet both sets of needs.

I noticed that Meg began to become more frightened of finding a job after she allowed herself to contemplate her childhood dream of becoming an artist. Realizing that she had a dream did not set her free; it only made her feel like more of a failure because not only was she unhappy in her current career, but also she hadn't had the courage to pursue what she really loved. This step of the process is very difficult and naturally leads to conflicting feelings. She was now not just jobless, she was a full-fledged failure both professionally and personally. She had a decision to make. She could either ignore her desire to pursue art one more time, or she could make a plan that would incorporate both sets of needs. We talked about her situation, and she decided that it wasn't yet time to pursue her dream. She simply asked me to help her to find another paralegal position. This time, however, she said that she wanted a job that didn't require as much overtime. I got the hint. She wanted time to think about what she was going to do and time to ease into making a change.

Meg was successful at finding a new job with less overtime, and for a while she seemed to be a little happier. About six months later, however, she called me and said that she was miserable even though the job didn't require much overtime. I asked her if she had done anything to pursue her art, and she said that she hadn't. I suggested that she might want to make one small step in that direction. Meg sounded annoyed and told me that it was her job that was the problem. I told her to keep me posted.

A few months later, Meg called to tell me that she had enrolled in an inexpensive drawing course taught by professional artists and that she was having a great time. She also told me that she was planning to take another drawing course the next semester and that she was thinking of trying to get a job in an art gallery so that she could be around art all the time. I told her that I thought her plan was a great idea. Within a year, Meg was working in a gallery and was continuing her artistic studies. Her goal is to have her own show within a few years.

Meg's story can be everyone's story. We don't need to make huge changes in our lives in order to pursue our dreams, and we don't need to do everything in one grand motion. We do, however, need to recognize that we are more than moneymaking machines, that we have dreams, and that our Souls have the right to express themselves in the material world. One small step leads to bigger steps which ultimately leads to dreams fulfilled.

THERE ARE NO ACCIDENTS: ALL NEEDS ARE FULFILLED

Sometimes what we call accidents can give us clues as to not only what we are asking life to give to us, but what our Souls might be urging us to do. In spiritual terms, what we call accidents are really events we do not understand due to a lack of complete knowledge about the way things work on the cosmic scale. Once we accept that we live in a lawful universe that is governed by the law of cause and effect, we can see that we create the circumstances in our lives based on what we have asked life to give to us.

When we look at our lives in an objective manner, we may find that we are enmeshed in situations that we cannot recollect having created. This is because we are unaware that we ask for things on both the conscious and unconscious levels. We may think that pursuing a certain career is the right thing to do because we have been told that it is, but our Souls, which are the guardians of our unconscious dreams, might have other ideas. We are divided within ourselves and don't even know it. Sometimes our Souls, and not our minds, urge us on by creating "failure" because it is the only way to shake us up and get us on the right track. The key is to become aware of our dreams and aspirations on a conscious level so that we can see why the so-called accidents of life occur and what they really mean.

I had just finished my junior year in college and didn't have a summer job lined up. I called the Federal Reserve Bank of Pittsburgh, where I had worked for several summers, and even though I wasn't thrilled at spending another summer doing mindless work that I had no interest in, I was confident that they could find a spot for me. When I learned that they couldn't give me a job, I was pretty shaken up, because I didn't have an alternative plan and I desperately needed money in order to survive during my last year of college. After several days of wracking my brain to figure out a way to make some money, the phone rang. It was the mother of a good friend of mine who wanted to know if I would be interested in looking after her elderly mother, Lydia, for the summer. Even though I had never worked in such a capacity before, I knew that I liked elderly people and I figured I had nothing to lose since the money was equal to what I would have earned at the bank.

I could go on forever about this job, but suffice it to say that working with Lydia was the best thing that ever happened to me. At the beginning, Lydia was not very easy to get along with. She was suffering from the aftereffects of a stroke, was on a lot of medication, and was not in the best of spirits most of the time. At first I treated her as if she were my patient and I knew what was good for her. But after a while I realized that I was on the wrong track. Something inside me told me that what she needed was not a caretaker, but a friend. I stopped acting like Supernurse and began treating her like a person. When she got angry and yelled at me, I yelled back at her. When she cried, I didn't ignore her feelings; I asked her to explain what was making her unhappy. Our relationship continued to develop, and by the end of the summer it dawned on me that I loved this ornery, frail little woman.

About halfway through the summer, I got another call out of the blue. I was asked to sing the lead in an original children's opera, something that I really wanted to do. Because my schedule with Lydia was flexible and because my friend's mother, for whom I worked, is a wonderful person, I was able to pursue my singing. I never would have been able to pursue this opportunity had I been working at the bank.

It took me many years to understand that my Soul had re-routed me that summer away from a job I didn't like but believed I needed, into a job that taught me that my future was working with people, not numbers. I also learned that it is possible to work and pursue creative and artistic aspirations at the same time.

NOT VICTIM, BUT VICTOR

The first key to becoming a victor is learning to practice patience. It is my personal belief that the world is populated by two types of people, the tortoises and the hares.

The tortoise and the hare are running a race. The hare, by nature, is the fastest of the two and is convinced that he will win the race if he just goes faster than the tortoise, which isn't too difficult. He doesn't find the race terribly challenging, however, so he wastes time by performing all sorts of tricks and taking many detours to convince himself and others not only how fast he is, but also just how clever he is. He expends so much energy in his efforts to prove his greatness that he loses sight of his goal, becomes tired, and falls asleep just before the finish line.

The tortoise, on the other hand, conserves his energy as he plods along, taking each step as it comes. He remains untroubled by the hare, who seems to be traveling the path faster than he is. Because he is guided by Spirit, he is unconcerned with outcomes. He knows that it is the journey that counts. He moves through rough terrain in the same manner as he moves through easy terrain, serenely, confidently. He knows that he'll reach his goal if he takes it easy and if he does what he is supposed to do. When he arrives at the finish line, the tortoise steps over the sleeping hare to victory. But even then he doesn't cheer for himself or ask for applause from the crowd. He turns back and pulls the sleeping hare across the finish line with him, simply because it is the right thing to do.

The second key to becoming a victor is adaptability, a beautiful lesson I learned from my mentors, Al and Jackie Kayata. Just as people are usually either hares or tortoises, they are also either orchids or weeds. Orchids are very beautiful and very sensitive and do not live a long time. In florist shops, they must be placed away from the other flowers and plants, in a climate-controlled environment, or they will wither and die. Weeds, however, are not beautiful in an ordinary way, but they flourish everywhere, even through the cracks in the sidewalk in the middle of urban jungles. When you pull them out, they grow back. They are oblivious to their external surroundings. They are fearless; they are adaptable; they cannot be destroyed.

Who are you, a tortoise or a hare, a weed or an orchid?

FOUR

HANDLING STRESS AND PRESSURE

Stress is one of the major reasons why most of us suffer from some degree of job dissatisfaction. Overwhelming stress and pressure prohibit us from truly enjoying our lives, affect both our physical and spiritual well-being, and exact a high toll. Because most of us have been conditioned to fear losing our jobs and are determined to do whatever is required so that this doesn't happen, we have lost sight of our most profound needs. In essence, we have become a society of slaves who value work above and beyond everything else and who go to great lengths to deny our spiritual natures. We see evolution only in economic and financial terms and deny any connection to our higher natures, our Souls, whose only desire is to lovingly guide us through our journey in material reality.

Stress and pressure begins at a young age. We believe that relaxation is bad, that only hard work is good, and that our children must get on the fast track as soon as they get out of diapers. Life, which should be a joyous process of discovery, be-comes a grind. We waste no time initiating our children into the grind by prodding them to get good grades, to get into a good high school or college, and then by convincing them to give up their dreams in favor of a bigger paycheck. We constantly remind them that if they want to get ahead, they have to stay ahead, and that means more hard work. We then wonder why everyone seems to be in a bad mood, living from vacation to vacation, holiday to holiday.

This is not the way that life has to be. It is possible to enjoy life and pursue our dreams while working at a job. The good news is that we don't have to wait until a heart attack or high blood pressure cuts us off at the knees to reevaluate our priorities. We can begin the reevaluation process this very moment. This instant we can begin to make the changes necessary to live more fulfilling lives.

My friend Linda and I went to high school together. Like many of our classmates, we were achievement-oriented and de-voted much time to getting ahead academically. What originally brought us together, however, was not academia, but our com-mon love of music and singing. When graduation time rolled around, we were surprised to find that we had both decided to attend women's colleges. We were lucky to have each other be-cause for some reason this decision seemed to separate us from most of our friends, who were heading off to coed institutions. We shared a common goal. We wanted to make it in the real world on our own terms. The problem was that we didn't know what "making it" really meant. We thought that because we were smart, we would succeed.

Interestingly enough, our college careers were also similar. Linda majored in English Literature, and I majored in French Literature. Our lives took a similar turn after graduation when Linda took a job working for a legal association while I began working in a law firm. It didn't take us long to realize that we had no real idea what we were doing. Even though our constant high level of stress proved just how hard we were working, and the fact that we could pay our rent proved that we were earning a living, we both knew that something was missing in our lives. This realization hit us both pretty hard, and our common search for meaning has been the cement of our friendship to this day.

Our lives continued to parallel each other. We both made preliminary ventures into spirituality as a way to close the gap in our lives. These first steps paid off. I realized that I wanted to work with people and was promoted into a management role at my firm, and Linda decided that she wanted to become a doctor.

The ramifications of Linda's decision were daunting. Because she had majored in English in college, she found herself facing an extra year of undergraduate study in the sciences just to be able to take the medical school entrance exams. She persevered, and even though she had to continue to work in order to pay for her extra schooling, her efforts paid off when she was accepted into medical school. We both thought we finally had it made. Little did we know that our journeys had just begun . . .

Linda, thirty-six, is now a family practice doctor working for an HMO. Prior to this position, she was on the faculty of a state university hospital. Before attending medical school, Linda considered herself a highly spiritual person and had experimented with meditation and alternative forms of healing. She went to medical school to combine her interests in both traditional and nontraditional methods of healing. Upon becoming a doctor, however, Linda realized that this was easier said than done.

"After I finished my residency, I had all but given up my spiritual pursuits. After being on call for shifts of up to twenty-four hours, practicing patience and compassion is the last thing that enters your mind. On one occasion I fell asleep as I was talking to a patient about her condition. After my residency, I took a job as a member of the faculty of the medical school, with responsibility for teaching, assisting in the management of a clinic, and seeing patients. I was under tremendous pressure and was constantly worried and stressed out. It wasn't until I was at the point of physical collapse that I realized that I had forgotten to take care of myself. I took a vacation, started meditating again, and began wondering why I had given up my spiritual practice.

"I came to the conclusion that the stress I was subjecting myself to was of my own doing and was not in keeping with my desire to be a healer. I found a new job as a doctor with an HMO. My current schedule is not entirely stress-free, but it does allow me to spend more time with my patients, to run and play volleyball, and to devote more energy to my spiritual interests. It's amazing, but the more I have become conscious of the needs of my Soul, the more effective I have become as a doctor and the more compassionate and patient I have become with others. I am now considering starting a medical practice with other doctors and healing professionals that would combine traditional Western medical care with alternative forms of healing."

THE REAL MEANING OF STRESS

When Linda first told me that even though she had reached her goal and was a well-respected physician, she was completely stressed out, I could only laugh. At this point in the game, I was no stranger to stress. It was evident that by completely dedicating our lives to achieving our goals, we had somehow missed the boat. We each had a choice to make. We could commiserate with each other until the end of time about how much pressure we were under, or we could try to figure out the reason for our circumstances and take steps to get off the fast track and get on the right track. Luckily we both decided on the latter course of action.

While it is obviously important to set goals and to take all of the steps necessary to achieve them, it is also important to keep them in their proper perspective. Sometimes we get so caught up in getting things done that we overwork our minds and neglect our Souls. And when we are blind to our spiritual needs, stress is the end result. In our society, stress has become a badge of honor worn to indicate that success has either been achieved or is imminent. We have all seen the devastating effects of stress in our own lives and in the lives of those with whom we work and live. It is not a pleasant sight.

I sometimes wonder how the historians of the future will judge our era. If someone had followed me around the workplace with a video camera during the first years of my career, he or she would have captured an otherwise intelligent person going about her tasks completely dominated by negativity, especially fear, anger, worry, and criticism. In fact, it was only recently that I fully understood how stress had affected me, when an old friend from my early working days remarked at how different I am now compared to how I used to be. When I asked her to elaborate, she proceeded by doing her imitation of me walking down the hall on any given day at work.

I watched in horror as she walked around my apartment, her shoulders hunched as if they were carrying the weight of the world, a scowl on her face and pain in her eyes, criticizing and barking orders to imaginary colleagues. I cringed at just how completely I had surrendered myself to stress for much of my career. The funny thing was, this wasn't simply an imitation of me. I was only doing what everyone else around me was doing to one degree or another. I was just another robot doing what I thought was necessary to prove my worth.

Why are we so stressed out? There are the external reasons

and then there are the internal reasons. The external reasons are obvious. Everyone else is doing it. There is not enough time in the day to meet the needs of our employers, our spouses, our children, and ourselves. With the advent of better technology, what could have gone out tomorrow by mail has to go out in an hour by fax. We are working longer and harder, yet we are producing and earning less. These pressures are real, but they are only a symptom of a deeper ill which is the result of our having forgotten that we are Souls who are on this Earth to live and learn, not simply to work.

When Linda realized that her level of stress was too high, she took a step back and found the courage to confront her predicament. She saw that in reality it was stress that was holding her back from achieving her dearest desire to become not simply a doctor, but a healer. It dawned on her that she had taken her true self out of the equation by giving up her power over her own life. She was no longer in charge of her destiny, and it was killing her.

Why do we give up our power over our lives? Because, in the short run, it is the easier route to take. I know from personal experience that it seems easier to buy into the ready-made version of reality promoted by most everyone we come into contact with than it is to risk seeking the answers to life's mysteries all alone. It appears easier to be a stressed-out victim than it is to be a free thinker who questions the rules of the game and refuses to turn over control to any person, place, situation, or thing.

A free thinker does not simply accept stress as a fact of life, but analyzes the reasons for its existence. The obvious reason for stress is that we have been trained from infancy to expect that things will not turn out for the best. We have been indoctrinated to believe that disaster is waiting around every corner and that the only solution is to be prepared for things to go wrong. With this deep and abiding fear firmly implanted in our minds, we have no other choice but to turn over our lives to the negative emotions that result from such an untenable psychological situation. We have no choice but to express anger, worry, and criticism.

But, despite what we might think, we do have a choice. We can choose whether or not to accept the premise that our reason for being is simply to get ahead at all costs in an attempt to avert disaster before it strikes, or the premise that we are here to live happy, productive, loving lives. The good news is that we do have a choice. The bad news is that many of us do not know it. We have become so accustomed to pain and stress that it has become our modus vivendi. We have completely surrendered ourselves to fear. Is it any wonder we cannot feel happiness?

Why would the divine power, whatever name you choose to give to it, create a self-conscious human being whose only job was to suffer? Why would this divine power provide us with the ability to feel the power of faith, if it did not expect us to access this emotion, at least in equal proportion to fear? We were endowed with self-consciousness and free will, yet most of us choose to remain stuck, using only one half of our emotions—the negative ones. The Soul is the power behind the mind, has access to a full range of emotions, and knows better.

The only requirement for happiness is to allow ourselves to access faith and to keep our "pain" in its proper perspective. How is it that some people who have undergone horrifying experiences such as being held captive against their will in concentration camps can be loving and forgiving Souls, while many of us, whose struggles pale in comparison, cannot even manage a kind word to our children or our spouse after a difficult day on the job? The answer is not as elusive as it may seem. Those people who have faced the unthinkable and have remained loving individuals have accessed their Souls, understand the power of Spirit, refuse to be sidetracked by fear, and know that life is good.

Every moment is a new opportunity to replace fear with faith, and even a tentative move in this direction will not go unrewarded. The realization will dawn that despite all evidence to the contrary on the material plane, we humans are here not to prove that we can take the worst life has to offer. We are not here to jump every manmade hurdle in a useless attempt to achieve our material goals at the expense of our well-being. We are here to recognize that we are powerful spiritual beings.

BALANCE IS THE KEY

Until only a few years ago, I was so determined to prove myself on the material level that I devoted every waking moment to work. I even devoted my non-waking hours to my fears about my job, and most of my dreams reflected this obsession. My work was literally consuming me twenty-four hours a day. If I wasn't planning the next day's agenda, I was worrying about what might happen to sidetrack me from meeting those all important deadlines.

At one point, I was suffering from chronic exhaustion and couldn't understand why I found it such a struggle to get out of bed in the morning. I went to see a doctor, and after a full battery of tests revealed that there was nothing physically wrong with me, the doctor told me I needed some balance. She suggested I begin by taking a vacation. I was relieved that I wasn't physically ill, but I wasn't thrilled when I realized that what I really needed was to completely overhaul my life.

Like Linda, I took a vacation. For the first few days, I was upset to realize that I couldn't relax even away from the stress and strain of my job. Eventually, however, as I began to unwind, the realization hit me that I had given up many of my interests and hobbies in order to pursue my career at a breakneck pace. I realized that all of my intensity on the job wasn't moving me forward; it was keeping me stuck in a life that I wasn't enjoying. I decided to make a list of the things that I had always wanted to do but hadn't been able to fit into my schedule. At the top of the list was my desire to sing. I began to cry because I had not done one thing to pursue my greatest pleasure.

Just as it is necessary to work and earn money, it is necessary to do what our Souls want us to do—that is, pursue the things that give us pleasure and bring pleasure to others. Even though there are few among us who would not disagree with this statement, many if not most of us deny ourselves happiness. Just as Linda got so caught up in doing what was expected of her as a doctor that she denied her loftier aspiration of being a healer. She found that it was impossible to be who she wanted to be— someone who cared, someone who spent time with her patients— if she did not take care of her own most profound needs.

As a society of workaholics, we have lost our way. When we do not give our minds a rest, when we do not take vacations because we fear that someone may step in during our absence and do a better job, when we worry that if we don't put in twelve-hour days we will lose our jobs, our life becomes nothing more than drudgery.

Most professionals are proud of the number of hours they put in at the office. I once worked with a lawyer who worked at least twelve hours a day, including weekends. She was so tense that she couldn't eat, and during the few years I was friendly with her she became thinner and thinner until I was afraid that her clothes were going to fall off her body. She was a very intelligent and warm person, but she was blind to any other aspect of her life other than work. She didn't have any hobbies, rarely took a lunch break to collect her thoughts, much less a vacation, and even though she had accomplished a great deal professionally, she was a mess. Her marriage fell apart, and to add insult to injury, she was asked to leave the firm. All she ever wanted was to "get ahead," but she neglected to ask herself where she was going.

This pain-oriented approach to life not only affects us as individuals, it negatively affects the future generations of our society. A good friend of mine once worked as an administrative assistant to Barbara, an ambitious, hardworking, and talented executive. Every afternoon at about 4:00 P.M. Barbara's daughter, who was in kindergarten at the time, would call to speak to her mother when she got home from school. And, of course, Barbara would speak to the child. If a client called when she was talking to her daughter, however, Barbara would not hesitate to put the child, and not the client, on hold, sometimes for long periods of time. Barbara was not deliberately trying to cause her little girl pain. She just couldn't seem to remember that a child is more important than a client.

One other example should suffice to make this point perfectly clear. My mother has been an elementary school music teacher for over twenty years. Recently, as school began, a little girl in her class told her that she felt ill. She told my mother that she felt sick to her stomach and thought that she might have a fever. After consoling the child, my mother called the girl's house, and her father promised to come pick her up. After about twenty minutes, the girl's father arrived and was very upset because he was late for work. My mother went back to her classroom, and a few hours later was shocked to find the little girl in the nurse's office, where she spent the rest of the day. It seems that both parents worked and neither of them felt that they could take the day off to be with their sick child, or take the time to make other arrangements so that the little girl could go home.

These stories, while not unusual, are a sad reflection of our times. These little children were learning the horrible lesson that work and stress take precedence over life. How long will it take before we see what we are doing to ourselves by not balancing our work and financial needs with our needs and responsibilities as spiritual beings? When will we stop making our lives and our children's lives a monument to stress and strain?

TAKING ACTION

If we want to get off the stress roller coaster, we must first have the courage to see that we have created the circumstances in our lives. We must understand that we, and not our employers, are responsible for our pain and then take the steps necessary to change the situation. Change is not easy. It is much easier to accept the status quo than it is to challenge our preconceived notions about the nature of reality; however, if we want to eliminate stress and live happy and contented lives, it is the only solution.

Why have we attracted stress into our lives? Because we are afraid to go against the tide and do what we want to do. We are surrounded by people who are not doing what they want to do with their lives. These people are in the majority and want nothing more than to have everyone else join them in their misery. Unfortunately many of these people are in positions of authority and like nothing better than to have willing victims under their control as they perpetrate the biggest lie of all: that in order for life to be meaningful, it has to be full of fear, pain, and stress.

Luckily, however, the status quo is changing thanks to those members of the human race who have dedicated themselves to spiritual principles rather than to economic principles. Each and every one of us is a unique creation of the divine. Each and every one of us has the inherent ability to make a positive contribution to the world in which we live by simply being who we are. It makes no difference whether our economic contribution to society is the result of driving a bus, typing a letter, or trading stocks and bonds. What matters is our spiritual contribution; that is, how we go about living our lives.

Linda realized that it wasn't enough for her to be a competent doctor who, due to her lack of physical and emotional energy, could only alleviate suffering by prescribing medication after a cursory meeting with her patients. She wanted to be a healer. Healers must be not only good doctors, but also compassionate people who care. Healers must have the time and the energy to develop a rapport with each person who comes to them for help. They must be able to build a bridge of trust with their patients if they truly want to heal. In order for Linda to heal others, she first had to heal herself.

If we want to heal ourselves, we have to trust that we are capable of change and then devote sufficient time for the healing process to work. We are instruments of the divine and as such have every right to make time for ourselves and for those we love. Why should fear stop us from taking an honest look at our lives and asking the hard questions? Let's push past whatever faulty ideas and negative emotions are holding us back and take the first step by making time to do the things that bring us pleasure.

Remarkable things will happen when we allow ourselves to take this first step. When I got back from that vacation, I forced myself (against my mind's judgment) to make time to sing. I spoke with my sister, a highly creative and motivated person, and we decided to put together an original musical revue to be performed at a local cabaret. I was nervous about my need to leave the office on time in order to rehearse, but strangely enough, my employers were very supportive of my need to sing. In fact, many of the people from my department came to the show and were very encouraging about my extracurricular life.

I was shocked when I realized that it was my fear and my

faulty assumptions about the people with whom I worked that had held me back from doing the things that I wanted to do. It wasn't my employer who was playing the role of the big, bad wolf; it was me all along. The funniest part of all is that even though I wasn't putting in a lot of overtime, I still got all my work done. In addition, because I had something to look forward to at the end of my workday, I was able to be a more lighthearted person on the job, and my level of stress significantly decreased. I still laugh to think that something so small—doing what I wanted to do—had such a huge affect on my level of happiness.

NOT ALL JOBS ARE CREATED EQUAL

Sometimes after we make the decision to enjoy our lives at the same time as performing our jobs, it becomes apparent that the job we have is not the right job. *Not* all jobs are created equal. Linda was faced with this situation when she realized that if she wanted to become a healer she would have to have a job that provided her with enough time to keep herself balanced and happy. She couldn't see patients, teach, and manage a clinic all at the same time. It was physically and emotionally impossible. She made the hard decision to find a new job that would fulfill her current needs.

As a headhunter, about one half of all the people I worked with told me that they were looking for new jobs because they were working too hard for too little return. Many of them were even open to considering jobs at less pay if they could work fewer hours or in less stressful environments. This is a step in the right direction, but fear stopped many of them from actually finding more suitable working environments. Many of us talk a good game, but when it comes time to step up to the plate, we find that it is more comfortable sitting on the bench.

Yet we all know that it isn't really all that comfortable staying a victim. It's actually quite draining. Our deepest dreams and aspirations will not go away because they are who we really are. It takes courage to venture out into the world as a Soul. It takes determination to replace fear with faith, because our trained, analytical, and stagnant minds undermine our best intentions.

Our minds constantly convince us that they know better. Stress isn't all bad, we say to ourselves. Stress and pressure make our egos feel important because at least we're doing something, anything. And, after all, who knows what may be lurking right around the corner at the next job? Maybe it won't be any better. Maybe it will be worse.

Maybe we should start trying to get what we want where we are now. Recently a good friend of mine decided that she wanted to work four days a week so that she'd have three days to pursue her musical career. After her decision was clear, she approached her employer with a viable plan to shorten her workweek. Her friends and colleagues were shocked at her bold move and did not hold out much hope for a positive outcome. Much to their surprise, my friend got exactly what she wanted, with no decrease in salary or benefits. Incredible? Not really. My friend was very skilled at her job, had very strong interpersonal skills, was always willing to learn something new, understood the needs of the business in which she worked, and could be relied upon to show good judgment. She knew that her plan was a win-win proposition—and so did her employer.

We must turn our attention away from the negative, destructive programming of our minds that endlessly tries to convince us that things can't get better and that the only appropriate response to life is fear, anger, worry, criticism, and stress. We must turn our attention to the life affirming, creative power of Spirit and to our Souls, which know that what we see and experience is simply a reflection of who we are at any given time.

Spirituality is about committing ourselves to a philosophy of life that is inclusive, nonjudgmental, and that values every person's expression of divinity. Spirituality is about recognizing that we are all one. Spiritual people encourage themselves, their children, and everyone else to pursue what has meaning and do not fool themselves into thinking that stress is proof of a job well done.

The point is, until we change ourselves, start doing what we want to do, and stop acting like victims, every job will be a stressful job. When we take back the control over our own lives, we begin to feel connected to something greater than a paycheck and can attract the right job to us. Most importantly, however, when we begin taking charge of our lives, we become able to express and receive the divine gifts of love, faith, patience, hope, duty, and compassion; and we know, beyond a shadow of a doubt, that life is good.

HARD TIME VS. GOOD TIME

The following seven steps can help to get us off the "stress express":

1. Step back from your current situation and look at it objectively. What's wrong with this picture?

2. Make a list of all your hobbies. When was the last time you made time to pursue them?

3. Make a list of all the things you have always wanted to do. What steps are you taking to actualize your dreams? What excuses are you using not to pursue your interests?

4. Be honest. How are you using stress to avoid what you really want to do?

5. How does stress make you act on and off the job? Are you full of fear? Do you worry constantly that you don't have enough time to get everything done? Do you make time to relax? If not, why not?

6. Suspend your disbelief and begin seeing yourself as a Soul, a unique expression of Spirit who is connected to the source of all life. How would this simple change in perspective alter your behavior? Imagine how you would act if you could eliminate stress from your life.

7. Is your job really keeping you from other worthwhile activities? If so, what is holding you back from finding a new job? What steps can you take now to attract a more suitable working environment?

FIVE

MAKE A SPIRITUAL RÉSUMÉ

At one point or another, most of us have had to create a résumé in order to get a job. A traditional résumé is a self-marketing tool to give a prospective employer the obvious reasons why he or she should hire you. This is well and good insofar as getting a job is concerned, but the problem is that after a certain point we begin to confuse who we are with what we do, and this is a big mistake.

Several years ago, I was taught this most important of lessons by a dear friend. I met him for the first time at a voice workshop, and while we were sitting at lunch, I turned to him and asked, "What do you do for a living?" He was clearly annoyed and responded, "I hate that question. What does what I do for a living have to do with anything? Let's talk about our love of music and singing instead, okay?" I was shocked but immediately saw his point. By this time, I had been studying spirituality for several years, but clearly I still wasn't able to separate what I did for a

79

living from who and what I was. In fact, I'm still trying to get the courage to walk up to a complete stranger at a party and say to him or her, "Hi, I'm Tami. What's your role in this vast universe of ours?"

Résumés don't really say anything about who we are above and beyond our educational background, what jobs we've held, and what work-related skills we've acquired along the way. They are superficial documents that portray only one aspect of our lives—our work lives. But, as we now know, we are much more than the sum total of our work experience. We are Souls, spiritual beings who are perpetually evolving, every second of every day.

In this chapter, you will be guided step by step as you create a different kind of résumé, a spiritual review of your inner world where who you are and what you believe to be true is more important than what you've done. Next, you will be asked to imagine your perfect job based on your spiritual beliefs. Finally, you will cross the bridge that separates your inner world from your outer world, and using your new spiritual insight and awareness, you will be able to uncover your Soul's hidden agenda with respect to your present career and work life.

Take as much time as you need with this chapter. There are no right or wrong answers to the questions that follow. This is not a test, and no one need ever see your answers. Take a few deep, slow breaths. Feel your body and mind becoming completely relaxed. Allow your Soul to guide you through this process of discovery. If you find yourself becoming blocked, take a walk or listen to some music. The answers will come to you when you are ready to hear them.

STEP 1: YOUR SPIRITUAL ORIENTATION

As we grow and evolve, so does our spiritual awareness. In this exercise, you will be asked to put your spiritual beliefs into words.

For many of us this is a difficult thing to do because of our past religious training. Affirming our own spiritual beliefs, even to ourselves, may feel uncomfortable because we are breaking with the religious or spiritual programming inculcated in us by our families, our church, and our culture as a whole. The key is *not* to think. Answer the following questions from your heart, not your mind. This first step is a work in progress. As you gain more spiritual insight and knowledge, your answers to the following questions will change. For the moment, however, we simply need to turn our complete attention to our inner world and temporarily forget everything else.

1. What is your conception of God or the Creator?

2. How do you personally define the word "Soul"?

3. What is the Soul's connection to God? What is your connection to God or the Creator?

4. Why is your life meaningful?

5. What brings you joy?

6. What is your definition of happiness?

7. On what spiritual principles do you base your life?

STEP 2: SOUL EXPERIENCE

We are so accustomed to thinking of ourselves as workers or professionals that we have forgotten that we are not on this planet simply to perform an economic function. The first step in counteracting this limiting belief is to give yourself total permission to think of yourself as a spiritual being who has experienced a full range of emotions and experiences intended to help you to

grow. Place your attention on your positive, life-affirming qualities and attributes and answer the following questions.

1. List all of your dreams and aspirations for your life. Do not
   judge whether they are appropriate, realizable, or practical.
   Just write them down.

2. As a Soul, you are unique and have many gifts and talents to
   offer the world. What are they?

3. Give examples of how you have positively used these gifts and
   talents in your life.

4. What is your definition of the following positive emotions and
   characteristics?
   > Faith
   > Kindness
   > Hope
   > Patience
   > Duty
   > Compassion
   > Love

5. Describe a situation from your life in which you naturally
   expressed each of the items on the preceding list. How did it
   feel to express them? How did your expression affect you, the
   other people involved in the situation, the situation itself?

STEP 3: SPIRITUAL OBJECTIVE FOR YOUR LIFE

Accept, if only for a moment, that your personal expression of
spiritual energy is of paramount importance to Life. It may seem
that you have been a ship without a rudder, blindly going about
your daily affairs, but this is not true. You are here, now, for a

reason. What is your spiritual mission in this lifetime? Why are *you* here on planet Earth?

STEP 4: IMAGINE YOUR PERFECT JOB

Based on your answers in Steps 1 to 3, suspend all practical and material considerations and allow yourself to imagine your perfect job, one that is leading you toward fulfilling one of your deepest dreams or aspirations for your life and is in keeping with your spiritual objective for your life. What would you be doing? How would you use your gifts and talents in service to the world? Imagine that it is possible to naturally express positive emotion in any situation with which you are confronted. How would you conduct yourself? How would you balance your time outside of work? How would you approach your relationships and your personal responsibilities? What hobbies or activities would you happily engage in?

STEP 5: THE BRIDGE

Sit quietly for a few moments. Relax your body and mind until you feel totally at peace. Immerse yourself in this feeling for as long as you can. Everything is perfect. Your life is perfect. You are perfectly healthy—physically, mentally, and spiritually. You are a perfect spiritual being with the power to change any negative circumstance into a positive opportunity for further spiritual growth. Imagine yourself crossing a bridge, the bridge between what you know to be true on the deepest spiritual level and the reality of the outer world. As you walk across the bridge, release all anxiety, tension, and fear about taking an honest inventory of your present life. You are a Soul, and no harm can come to you.

When you feel ready, step off the bridge into the outer world. You are totally at peace with yourself and are completely willing and able to see the life you've created for yourself, knowing that you have the power to change and grow.

STEP 6: LIFE REVIEW—YOUR EDUCATION

Think back to your high school, post–high school vocational training, college, and graduate or professional school days. If your answers to the following questions seem to be "negative," don't let this concern you at this point. Don't be afraid to be honest. Our goal in the next two steps is to uncover the beliefs that you have about yourself and the circumstances that are holding you back from achieving your dreams and aspirations. Let go. These erroneous beliefs and seemingly negative experiences are not set in stone and are only the Soul's way of letting you know what you must do to fulfill your destiny as a spiritual being.

1. Who made the decisions regarding where you went to school and what course of study you pursued? Was it your parents or guardians, other people in authority, or did you make the decision? How have these decisions affected your life?

2. What general feelings do you have about your educational experiences? Did you enjoy school, hate it, or were you indifferent? Were you the sort of person who enjoyed extracurricular activities, such as sports, clubs, theatrical productions, etc., more than the academic subjects? Were you outgoing or were you shy and retiring?

3. What were your greatest accomplishments during your school years?

4. What were your greatest disappointments during your school years?

5. What is your underlying belief regarding your level of education? Do you feel that you received too much education, didn't receive enough education, weren't encouraged to pursue higher education, are happy with the level of education that you have?

6. Knowing what you know now, if you could go back and change your educational experience in any way, what would you do differently? Why?

7. Have you continued your education since leaving school? If not, why?

STEP 7: LIFE REVIEW—YOUR WORK EXPERIENCE

Now, turn your attention to your work experiences. Every job counts, including summer, temporary, and volunteer work. Once again, don't be afraid to be "negative" when answering the following questions. This exercise is not about getting a job; it's about finding out what you believe to be true about your work life to date.

1. What made you choose the fields of work you've pursued? Were these fields of work your idea or someone else's? Have you pursued the fields of work that hold the most interest for you, or has your decision simply been the result of your need to make money to support yourself?

2. What are your general feelings about the direction your work has taken? Are you happy with the fields of work you've pursued? Why or why not? Which jobs have brought you the

most pleasure? Why? What jobs have been unsatisfying? Why?

3. What have been your greatest work-related accomplishments so far?

4. What have been your greatest work-related disappointments so far?

5. What is your underlying belief regarding your work experiences to date? Have you been adequately compensated for the work you've done? Have you been well respected and well treated in your jobs? Has it been difficult or easy for you to find satisfying work? Do you feel as if you're getting ahead, or just treading water in your career?

6. Knowing what you know now, what would you have done differently to make your work experiences more fulfilling? What can you do to make your current job more fulfilling?

STEP 8: LIFE REVIEW—PATTERNS

Life is not a series of unrelated, confusing events. There is a direct correlation between what we believe to be true about ourselves and what happens in material reality. Our lives have unfolded based on patterns that have emerged as a result of our deepest, unconscious beliefs. If we want to move forward in a more positive direction, we must uncover the patterns that are keeping us stuck in place. The only requirement for this exercise is an open mind and heart and a willingness to see your role in creating the circumstances you currently face. As you answer the following questions, keep reviewing your answers to the questions in Steps 6 and 7 and allow yourself to see the interconnection between your thoughts, your beliefs, and your reality.

1. Have you been heavily influenced by others in making decisions about your education? Your choice of jobs? If so, explain how this makes you feel and why you think this has occurred.

2. Have you pursued the fields that hold the most interest for you? If not, why not?

3. Have you made the most of every job you've had?

   a. Have you developed professional and personal relationships that you still maintain from the jobs you've had? If so, how have these relationships affected your life? Have these relationships played any role in helping you to find other jobs? If not, why not?

   b. Did you take advantage of everything your employers had to offer (e.g., career counseling, continuing education programs, skill development courses, management training programs)? If you did, what opportunities did you take advantage of? If not, why have you not pursued these opportunities?

   c. Did you have a mentor on the job (i.e., someone who took an interest in your work and guided you along the way)? If so, how did your mentor help you along the way?

   d. Did you act as a mentor to anyone at this job? If not, why not? If you did, how did acting as a mentor to another person make you feel? What effect did your role as a mentor have on your life?

   e. Have you stayed in one job longer than you think you should have? Why? If you have moved around a lot, what has prompted you to do so?

4. Is there a pattern that emerges with respect to your reasons for changing jobs? Did you leave most of your jobs to make more money? Are you easily bored? Have you always worked in the same job? Are you afraid of moving forward to the next level? Are you hesitant about taking advantage of opportunities that may be available to you at your current job?

5. Is there a common denominator between your greatest educational disappointments and your greatest work-related disappointments? How about between your greatest educational achievements and your greatest work-related achievements? What do you think this means?

6. Is there a common denominator between your underlying belief about your education and your work experiences? What do you think this means? If you are dissatisfied with the way your work life has progressed, what do you think the underlying reason is for your dissatisfaction?

STEP 9: LIFE REVIEW—FEAR

Even the most self-evolved among us are victimized by fear from time to time. If your answers in Step 8 did not reveal a series of underlying fears related to your work situation, you probably aren't being totally honest with yourself. This is not surprising. It isn't easy to be honest about fear. Even after many years of spiritual exploration, I couldn't make the connection between my own fears and my dissatisfaction with my life. One day several years ago in a session with a trained rebirther, I had the first in a series of revelations that led me to understand the connection between what I believed and the reality of my life.

Rebirthing is a breathing technique that is intended to help the client to relive the moment of birth in an effort to release any traumatic or negative feelings associated with the event. I didn't "relive" my birth in this session; that happened much later, but during this session I found myself traveling through space, weightless and at peace. As I was returning to ordinary reality and my breathing returned to normal, I was shocked to find that I was sobbing uncontrollably. When my rebirther asked me to explain what I was feeling, I told her that I realized that what was holding me back from living my ideal life was my belief that the people in my life never adequately supported me, nor would support me, in my quest to achieve my goals and aspirations.

When I got home that night, I realized that this belief was making me afraid to succeed. I then mustered up the courage to go a step further. Why would I be so afraid of success? I was well educated, talented, well liked, and making good money. I knew that I had always been promoted at every job I had ever had and had many achievements to my credit. What was going on here? Then it dawned on me. I was afraid because for a long time something inside me had been urging me not to take the conventional road to professional success, not to be so concerned with gratifying my own ego, but to travel the spiritual path. Then it hit me. If I was going to devote my life to the spiritual path, I would have to travel alone. I would have to be my own support. I would have to have faith and turn my life over to something greater than myself, something greater than the power of fear.

1. Have you fulfilled any of your dreams and aspirations from Step 2? If yes, what dreams or aspirations have you achieved and how did it make you feel to fulfill them?

2. Regardless of whether you have or have not fulfilled any of your dreams from Step 1, list the dreams and aspirations you would still like to fulfill.

3. Review your answers to 2 above. List all of the obstacles that are standing between you and the fulfillment of your dreams.

4. Make a list of all of your fears related to fulfilling your dreams.

5. Next to each fear, write down how each of these fears has manifested itself into a work-related weakness. For example, my fear of not being supported resulted in my constant need for approval on the job. This was a weakness because I had difficulty making decisions on my own.

STEP 10: TRANSMUTATION

1. Take your list of fears and weaknesses and look at them objectively. Are they logical based on what you now know about yourself as a spiritual being?

2. Weaknesses and fears are simply strengths waiting to emerge from the shadows. Take each of your fears or weaknesses and describe how they can be transformed into strengths by applying one or more positive feelings (faith, hope, kindness, compassion, duty, love, and patience). For example, my fear of not being supported is transmuted into a strength through the application of faith. When I feel afraid that I may not receive adequate support for a decision I must make, I can choose to have faith that, as a spiritual being, I have the courage to stand alone.

3. Take a look at your underlying beliefs about your education and your work experience. How can these beliefs be trans-

muted by applying one or more positive feelings? For example, if my underlying belief about my education and work experiences is that I do not have enough education and I am never given challenging work on the job, I can transmute these beliefs by applying love, faith, and patience. The new belief becomes: I love, respect, and am grateful for the level of education I have received. I am open to new educational opportunities and have faith that if I exhibit patience, challenging work opportunities will manifest in my life.

4. Now take a look at the patterns that emerged from Step 8. Apply the same process that you used for your fears and weaknesses and for your underlying beliefs to transmute these patterns into positive statements. For example, if I always leave jobs out of boredom, I can transmute this pattern by applying patience and duty. The transmutation would then become: I am a patient person whose life is meaningful. Therefore, any work that I do is meaningful and necessary. I am a Soul and as such have a duty and a responsibility to fulfill my spiritual destiny. I am open to new challenges and opportunities, and they continually manifest themselves in my life.

STEP 11: SOUL WORK

Accept, if only for this exercise, that everything you have ever done is meaningful, that nothing happens by chance, and that you are completely responsible for the choices you have made and for the circumstances in your life.

Suspend your disbelief and draft a narrative explaining your educational and work history from your Soul's perspective, i.e., that all your educational and work experiences have been positive because they have taught you the lessons you needed to learn in order to reunite with your Soul. Let your imagination be your guide, and explain how all of your experiences have been leading you toward the realization of your dreams and aspirations. Include any "coincidences" that led you to a particular course of study or a particular job and what messages from your Soul were hiding in these seemingly random events. Have fun with this exercise and feel the power that comes when you choose to see your life in a different light.

STEP 12: MISSION STATEMENT

We have come to the conclusion of this part of our journey. The only thing left for you to do is to fill in the following blanks in the statement below. Read this statement aloud to yourself at least once a day and any time you feel lost and without purpose. It will bring you home.

I am first and foremost a spiritual being. My life is meaningful and has purpose. I am a Soul and have the power to change negative circumstances into positive opportunities at will. With faith, love, hope, duty, compassion, patience, and kindness, I pursue my spiritual objective which is (look back at your answer in step 3) _____. As a Soul, I am a unique expression of Spirit/God or the Creator and have many gifts and talents to offer the world, including (look back at your answer in Step 2) _____. As a Soul, I am able at any time to step back from external reality, reconnect with my inner world, and bask in my spiritual essence. My life is proceeding perfectly toward the realization of my dreams and aspirations. In fact, I am already there.

PART THREE

ALL THE WORLD'S
A STAGE

YOU ARE THE LIGHT

Fast and furious
The candle burns
without the wax
Vast and curious
You look at me
like I can't relax
Wondering who I am
I face myself and ask the past
"Who are you," said I
A child answers in the sky
"You are the light"

—PETER SCHAUFELE

SIX

DEALING WITH AN IMPOSSIBLE BOSS

Thus far on our spiritual journey we have tackled some heavy issues, and we can see how the thoughts we think and the emotions we choose to express in any given situation affect our external reality. We have seen that because we are Souls, and not simply minds with bodies, we have the power to transmute negative circumstances into positive opportunities and that it is possible to find meaning in a job well done, to cope with layoffs and other job-related failures, and to handle stress and pressure. We now know that we have created and are responsible for the quality of our work lives, as well as our lives as a whole.

Now the time has come to bring our relationships with other people into the equation. Most people can accept to one degree or another that they are responsible for the external circumstances in their lives and that it is possible to change these circumstances by adopting a more positive attitude, but shrink at the notion that they can profoundly transform their relationships, on or off the job, by using a spiritually oriented approach. Why? Because they do not truly understand that on the most basic of levels, there is only one life—Spirit—and that everyone they ever deal with is simply an aspect of themselves crying out for recognition, acceptance, love, and ultimately transformation.

Even after I had been actively pursuing the spiritual path for ten years, I refused to see that I was responsible for attracting the people in my life in the same exact manner that I had attracted my life circumstances in order to evolve as a spiritual being. I could accept that my life was my own creation, but assumed that other people came across my path by accident. How could it be my doing if several of the bosses I had were angry, impossible monsters who were out to sabotage my kindly, spiritual nature? Surely this was due to some spiritual loophole of which I was unaware. What a shock it was to realize that no such loophole existed and that the monsters I worked for represented aspects of my own personality that I did not wish to confront.

As I have said before, my saving grace has always been my limited ability to cope with misery and pain. Eventually, when things get bad enough and I can't rationalize feeling horrible any longer, I turn inward in a last-ditch effort to make sense of the pain. On one such occasion, I had a flash of insight when I realized that if there was one negative emotion to which I was particularly attached, it was anger, the by-product of my deep and abiding fear of not being in control of my life. Mysteriously enough, I also had a difficult time showing patience when faced with this fear. Some divine, beneficent force smiled on me that day, because suddenly I saw without a doubt that all of the people with whom I had difficulty shared this same problem.

I do not think that I am the only one on the planet who has a problem with anger. I know that I am in very good company. My evidence for this is the fact that our external world is full of war, violence, and crime. It is only necessary to open the morning paper to see the legions of new victims who surface each day crying out in rage against the injustices committed against them. Is it any wonder why the workplace has become a battlefield?

There are few among us who have not felt the direct and indirect effects of an angry or irresponsible boss berating us, yelling at us, and thwarting our efforts at every turn. There are even fewer who have not felt angry, critical, and hateful in the face of such circumstances. Even the most composed and evolved of our species find it difficult to return to their homes after a full day of hell and resist the temptation to recreate this same hell with family and friends.

The problem is that we have become too comfortable with our role as victims, trained as we are to believe that anger and fear are the only appropriate responses to the negative aspects of life. We have been indoctrinated, against our better spiritual judgment, to accept our mind's conclusion that we are destined to remain on this treadmill forever. Worse, we erroneously think that the only way to deal with negative situations and people is to "grin and bear it" or to "fight fire with fire." Fortunately, however, there is another way to view the anger-fear predicament we face each and every day.

Jonathan, age thirty, is a marketing director in an accounting firm. On his first day on the job, he was greeted with warnings from his colleagues to be careful of Ed, his new boss, as he was the most impossible person in the firm. Ed was referred to as "Old Faithful" due to his frequent outbursts of anger and rage, and as "the hatchet man" due to his penchant for firing people who worked for him. Ed reminded Jonathan of his father, with whom he had a difficult and volatile relationship.

"I must admit that I was not a happy camper those first few weeks. My new boss was everything my coworkers told me he would be. I was filled with fear every time I had to ask him a question and I dreaded our weekly status meetings. I decided, however, that I was either going to confront this fear in myself and try to understand Ed and empathize with him, or I would not be able to succeed at a job that I loved."

After a few weeks of not-so-pleasant treatment, Jonathan decided that he would have to confront the situation. Despite recommendations from his friends and colleagues to "let the old guy have it," Jonathan decided that he could not counteract Ed's negative attributes with further negativity. Instead, he decided to counteract any of Ed's negative statements or actions with a positive statement or action of equal force.

"I realized that my boss was in pain, or he wouldn't be acting this way, and that the only way to improve myself and the situation was to show compassion. When he was angry, I asked him why he was angry and what we could do together to improve the situation. I would thank him for any advice or information he provided me with and made it clear that I had much to learn from him. In essence, I constantly appealed to his higher self and to the positive attributes that I knew were hidden behind his negative behavior.

"After a few weeks of using this new approach, I realized that Ed wasn't the only one with a problem. As a result of my fear of anger, I had repressed my own feelings of anger. I decided that I had to make peace with this powerful emotion. Whenever I felt angry, I applied the same patience and compassion I showed to Ed to myself. It didn't happen overnight, and it wasn't always easy, but within a few months my relationship with Ed had significantly improved. I also found myself managing the people who worked for me in a more positive manner. Strangely enough, my relationship with my father is also improving."

ACKNOWLEDGING THE MIND'S REACTION

The mind's reaction to Jonathan's story goes something like this: *Jonathan should have given Ed a good swift kick in the butt. I guess some people can't help being doormats. He'll never get ahead by being nice. Doesn't he understand that kindness is weakness?* The mind does not want to believe in the power of positive emotion, or in the Soul, because the Soul threatens the mind's role as "command central." The mind is used to fear. It has come to like the status quo. It doesn't want to trade in fear for faith, anger for patience, criticism for compassion, or hatred for love. It wants vengeance and finds relief in the old adage "Don't get mad, get even." But what if we are tired of being ruled by fear? What if we don't want to live by the sword? What if we want peace, internally and externally? What do we do? Let's get some clues from Jonathan's story.

ENTERING THE LION'S DEN

The first thing that Jonathan did was the same thing he had done a thousand times before. He entered the lion's den of external reality. In this case, external reality was the workplace. His co-workers, like most of us, were experts at the fear game and warned him that he was in for trouble. He would be working for the most horrible boss in the whole company. Jonathan's mind immediately prejudged the situation as dangerous, kicked into action by selecting anger, criticism, and hatred as his weapons, and directed his muscles to tense up in preparation for the battle ahead. He played imaginary scenes over and over in his mind to prepare himself to deal with Ed, "Old Faithful," "the hatchet man." He was mentally prepared for the worst-case scenario, and just like magic, the worst-case scenario materialized before him. His mind told him that he was powerless to control the situation, that he was now Ed's victim. For several weeks, all he could do was grin and bear it. In his words, he was "not a happy camper."

How many times has this or a similar scenario played out in your own life? Speaking for myself, I lost count about a week into my first job. To be honest, I think Jonathan handled those first few weeks with Ed rather well. To his credit, he didn't victimize anyone but himself with his feelings of anger, criticism, and hatred. I can't remember how many times I have criticized a coworker, lost my temper with a secretary, or spent an hour on the phone with a friend venting my intense feelings of hatred after a run-in with a difficult boss. Of course, I felt badly about my behavior, but I didn't question my "right" to act out my negative emotions and ruin everyone else's day. How many times do we have to repeat the same scenario before we see the fear game for what it is: an endless cycle of misery?

UNCOVERING OUR BELIEFS

This cycle of misery is the result of giving our mind full reign over our belief system and over our behavior. The mind has been conditioned by the events and experiences of the past and has created a belief structure to make sense of these experiences. This belief structure has been a useful guide in helping us to navigate through stormy waters. But in essence it is a trap: Our past experiences shape our beliefs which shape our experiences which, in turn, provide experiential proof of the validity of our beliefs. To use a simple example, if as a child I was told by someone in a position of authority that I wasn't good in math, I probably accepted this as a foregone conclusion, didn't work very hard in math class, and consequently didn't learn much math. The fact that later on in my life I experienced difficulty balancing my checkbook only served to reinforce my belief that I wasn't good in math. There is, however, a way out of this trap. The first step is to take a good look at the people and the circumstances in our lives that are causing us to suffer and then uncover the beliefs that are attracting them to us.

Jonathan gets a flash of insight when his mind reveals to him that Ed and his father share similar characteristics. He makes the connection that his volatile and difficult relationship with his father has something to do with his current predicament with Ed. He can either use this information to reinforce his belief that all men in authority are angry and impossible like his father and respond to Ed the same way he has always responded to his father; or he can use this insight to get to the heart of why angry and impossible men are recurring characters in his own personal drama; take responsibility for his role in creating the drama; and finally, take the steps necessary to change the script.

It doesn't take years of intensive psychoanalysis to understand that much of our personality is shaped in childhood. In fact, our childhood experiences form the foundation of our beliefs about the world. If either or both of our parents or caregivers reacted to the events and circumstances of their lives or to us with anger, criticism, or hatred, as children we probably felt afraid and powerless. As a result of feeling afraid and powerless, we either reacted to the world around us and to the events in our own lives with anger, criticism, and hatred, or repressed our feelings altogether. In any case, we surely did not see the world as a nurturing, compassionate, loving place. Instead we became, like most everyone else, expert players in the fear game.

The fear-anger-criticism-hatred pattern formed in childhood results in a belief structure that strongly influences the events and circumstances of our lives right through adulthood, including on the job. From a psychological perspective, Jonathan's relationship with Ed serves as a stand-in for Jonathan's relationship with his father. From a spiritual perspective, Jonathan has attracted what he fears the most. He has not done this to punish himself, but to give him an opportunity to uncover his belief that all men are angry and impossible and to take the steps necessary to heal himself from the ramifications of this belief.

RECOGNIZING, NOT REPRESSING, FEAR

By recognizing that he has attracted the situation with Ed to himself through his belief that all men are angry and impossible, Jonathan has taken responsibility for playing a role in creating the situation. By taking responsibility for attracting the situation, he is no longer a powerless victim of fate. When we repress our fears, the mind has no alternative but to respond to the situation in the same way it has responded a million times before—in a knee-jerk fashion. This is the mind's way of protecting us. This "protection" from angry people served us well as children, but as we mature it blocks us from greater understanding. By recognizing the fear and uncovering its source, Jonathan can use his reason to decide how he wants to respond to this emotion in the present moment.

FIGHT OR FLIGHT

When confronted with the negative emotion of fear, the mind, in conjunction with the body, must first make the decision whether to flee or to stay and fight. While Jonathan still feels fear, he analyzes the level of danger in the situation and makes the decision to stay and fight. Of course, there are times when the only appropriate response to fear is to get out of harm's way.

When confronted with the threat of physical or intense emotional violence, one must exercise the best possible option to ensure survival. Not every confrontation with fear is a call for battle. In my experience in the work world and in counseling and helping people to find jobs, however, I have found that most people who have a problem coping with fear or anger take the first chance they can to leave their jobs when confronted with an emotionally charged relationship such as an angry, "impossible" boss.

I myself have exercised this option on more than one occasion. Yet, I have found in most cases, including my own, that a similar emotionally charged relationship is waiting for them at the next job and the next until the fear is confronted. By choosing to stay and fight, you are taking the first steps to conquering your fear and to eliminating the need for these negative situations and re-lationships to reappear on the external stage.

Don't worry if you fail or cannot make the leap in one fell swoop. Every experience is a learning experience with some in-sight to be gained. You will encounter a similar situation some-where else, perhaps in less painful and more manageable circumstances where you will eventually confront the fear.

DECIDING TO RESPOND THROUGH THE MIND OR THROUGH THE SOUL

Up until this point, Jonathan has used the power of his mind to assess his current situation with Ed. He is now faced with the *choice* of whether to respond to Ed through his mind or through his Soul. This is a very difficult decision for Jonathan because his mind will try anything to get him to follow its lead and respond to Ed with the same negative emotions that Ed is exhibiting toward him. His decision is further complicated because he, like the rest of us, is not used to asking his Soul for guidance or to implementing its advice. Jonathan is not sure that he will be able to hear his Soul's message.

We have difficulty hearing the Soul's message because we see the Soul as some small part of us and not as the essence of who we are. When we change our conception of the Soul—from seeing ourselves as having a Soul to seeing ourselves as living Souls—it becomes easier and easier to make direct contact with our spiritual natures.

We must constantly remind ourselves that on the most basic of levels, *everything* in the universe is pure energy or Spirit. Thus, since everything is formed from and is a manifestation of energy or Spirit, energy or Spirit is really all that exists. As Souls we are directly connected to this energy or Spirit and are conduits through which this energy or Spirit moves and changes as it creates the circumstances of our lives. Just as the Soul is the link to energy or Spirit, reason is the link between the mind and the Soul.

Let's return to Jonathan's story for a minute. When Jonathan understands that there is a similarity between his relationship with his father and his relationship with Ed, it is his reason that provides him with this insight. Now, there are two kinds of reason. One kind of reason is the type that is completely influenced by belief and uses the experiences of the past to make sense of the present. This reasoning ability is the mind's way of protecting us from the painful effects of fear. But if you think about it, this kind of reason only has the ability to recreate the past over and over each and every day. It has no connection to anything beyond itself.

The other type of reason is intuitive. This kind of reason is accessed every day without our being aware of it. Think about it. Have you relied on gut feeling? Have you ever done something for no apparent reason other than "it felt like the right thing to do"? When this happens, it is as if our usual reasoning ability is temporarily short-circuited, and another faculty seems to be "running the show." Intuition is the voice of the Soul and is constantly flooding our minds with ideas, solutions, and suggestions. We can hear it when the mind is quiet. Intuition bypasses our beliefs and our experiences and immediately connects us with our own inner world where Spirit, the source of all creation, resides.

We can think of the mind and the Soul as two radio stations constantly broadcasting in our heads. When we believe that we are mental-physical but not spiritual beings, the mind's station comes in loud and clear and can be heard all the time, while the Soul's station comes in very faintly, is clouded by static, and is hard to hear. If we want to tune into the Soul's message, we have to lower the volume on the mind's message. The Soul's message to Jonathan is clear. In order to confront and change his current situation with Ed, Jonathan must replace his feelings of fear with faith, anger with patience, criticism with compassion, and hatred with love.

The choice to go against your mind, your cherished beliefs, and your personal history in favor of the advice of your Soul is an act of ultimate faith and is probably one of the most courageous things anyone can ever do. Leaving the secure landscape of the mind in favor of the uncharted territory of the Soul is an extremely difficult decision, but ultimately if we want to end the cycle of misery, it is the only thing to do. You may have to confront some uncomfortable truths about yourself and your experiences. At first you may feel as if you have landed all alone in a foreign country where everyone except you speaks the same language. It is frustrating and at times galling. There may not be immediate results—you have difficulty making yourself understood, people react strangely to you, and your body may react to the stress of being a stranger in a strange land.

I remember the first time that I consciously decided to express patience instead of anger. I had a few friends over for dinner, and we discussed politics. Every time I tried to interject my thoughts and opinions, one of my guests would cut me off and belittle what I was saying. I felt angry, and my mind urged me to release the emotion and "let my friend have it." It was as if there were a huge battle between two superpowers going on inside my head. Against my mind's judgment, I decided to listen to my Soul, to remain calm and patient and to try to see the situation as an observer rather than as a participant. I was feeling pretty proud of myself when I started feeling intensely itchy. I still refused to become angry. The itching continued. I went into the bathroom and noticed that the entire upper half of my body had broken out in hives. I chuckled softly, saluted my mind's power of persuasion, and returned to my guests. Finally my friends decided that it was time to go home. About five minutes after they left, the hives disappeared.

The same hives reappeared the following night during dinner with another friend. I recognized my anger but persisted in showing patience and compassion. As I have become more comfortable expressing patience in trying circumstances, the outbreaks of hives have lessened greatly and now only serve to remind me that I have not as yet completely eliminated anger from my life.

The mind will try to intervene, will try to convince you that you need not be all alone, that you can always go back to your old ways and your old friend "negative emotion." If you are persistent, however, and keep picking yourself up each time that you fall down, you will succeed and will flourish in your new environment. The misery and unhappiness of the past will be but a memory, and remarkable things will happen. You will see the Eds of the world, and everyone else, as the Souls that they really are, struggling just like you, on the road to peace.

PATIENCE, COMPASSION, AND LOVE

What does it really mean to express positive emotion? Let's first start with what it doesn't mean. It doesn't mean that you simply shut up and swallow your feelings. It doesn't mean that you keep silent when you disagree with someone. It doesn't mean that you become a yes-man or -woman and do the boss's bidding like some zombie in a horror film. It doesn't mean that you stop doing your job.

It does mean that you remain "in the world but not of it," by not taking personally whatever situation or people you are confronted with. It does mean that even if you disagree with your boss's or anyone else's opinions or actions, you remain centered and resist the temptation to judge him or her. It does mean that you look behind the expression of negative emotion to find the inner power waiting there to reconnect you to the realm of Spirit, the ground of being. It does mean that you only interact with the Soul of any individual in any situation.

Negative energy is dark, and darkness can only be dispelled by light. The light of positive emotion is strong and has the power to change the situation, even if its effects are not immediately apparent.

When a boss is overly critical of our work, tries to undermine our self-esteem and self-worth through expressions of anger, and is generally prone to the dark side of human emotion, we must find the courage to step back from the situation, disengage our mental apparatus, and allow ourselves to understand the situation as a reflection of the boss's state of being. Any person who spends a great deal of time criticizing and demeaning the work of others is obviously not a happy person, has probably been the victim of ruthless criticism, is constantly judging him- or herself and others, and does not see the world as a place where his or her needs are being met. Will it honestly help the situation to add more fuel to the fire? Wouldn't we see the situation differently if we had faith that the universe is inherently good and that as a Soul we have the ability to connect with Spirit? Wouldn't the situation be transformed if we were able to be patient, compassionate, and loving enough to see the boss as a Soul struggling to understand its own process and then forgive his or her negative behavior?

This does not mean that we need to sit there with a martyred look on our face. It means that we should look beyond the messenger and see the message. Is there *any* truth to the criticism of our work expressed by our boss? If so, wouldn't it be honest, and perhaps shocking, to verbalize whatever validity there was to the criticism and then to solicit constructive advice about how to improve the work product? Why can't we teach the boss how to help us by asking him or her to assist us in improving the product? When we refuse to react to the negative aspect of any situation and act as a Soul by applying positive energy, we are confronting the situation in a constructive manner. We effectively disarm the person exhibiting the negative behavior and leave him or her sitting in a little less darkness than before.

We all stand for something. We can either stand for negativity and destruction or we can stand for the positive, life-affirming beauty inherent in each one of us and in the world around us. The next time you are confronted with a disagreeable, negative personality, remember the choice is up to you.

RECOGNIZING THAT THE BATTLE IS WITHIN

Jonathan's final realization comes when he realizes that Ed is not the only one who has a problem with anger. He realizes that he, too, has this same problem, even though he does not express the emotions outwardly. He understands that the battle he is waging with Ed is really the outer reflection of the battle he is with himself. He comes to terms with the ultimate reality that he alone is responsible for the circumstances of his life. By accepting that the battle is always within, Jonathan is no longer a powerless victim. By changing the way he responds to external circumstances, and by applying the same compassion, patience, and love he has shown to Ed to himself, Jonathan has taken a major step in changing himself.

It is very easy to blame our parents, our teachers, or others who had authority over us in our youth for our problems. It would be very convenient and rational from the mind's perspective for Jonathan to blame the whole situation with Ed on his father. But where would this blame stop? Jonathan's father could surely trace his problem with anger back to his father, and Jonathan's father's father could do likewise, ad infinitum. The first step is to look at our present reality to find clues about the beliefs that shaped this reality and then to find out where these beliefs originate. If we stop there, however, and do not go the extra mile to forgive the past by taking responsibility for the present, we are *not* acting as Souls. As spiritual beings, we can access the perspective and wisdom of eternity because we are connected to all that is. From this vantage point, there is no blame—there is only Spirit.

A miraculous thing happens once Jonathan lets go of blame and begins practicing patience, compassion, and love. After a few months of constant effort, his relationships with Ed, with the people he manages, and with his father start to improve. Jonathan now knows that if he wants to make further changes in his life, all he has to do is change himself first.

The time has now come to say good-bye to Jonathan and turn the flashlight on ourselves.

SEVEN

COPING WITH AN INSECURE COLLEAGUE

Our bosses are not the only ones who try our patience on the job. Many times it is an insecure colleague who pushes us to the limits of our endurance, threatening to drive us completely crazy. When I first entered the workforce out of college, it seemed as if my workplace was completely populated by insecure people. It didn't appear to me as if my colleagues were engaged in a collaborative effort for the common good. Rather, it seemed to me that every man or woman was out for him- or herself, plotting and scheming either how to get the more high-profile assignments or, alternatively, how to keep a low profile in order to avoid challenging work.

What I didn't understand at the time was that those insecure people were only reflecting my own state of mind back to me. The first months of my first job after college were very difficult. Just a few months prior to gaining this position, I was a successful student. My time was my own. I knew my way around the campus and I had a million friends. As graduation came and went, so did the secure lifestyle that had taken me four years to build. Suddenly I was in New York City, I didn't have any money, I needed an apartment, and I didn't know very many people.

At work I was the new kid on the block, so naturally I didn't get the best assignments. For several months, the only project I had to work on was organizing the files for a major case that included many thousands of documents. Not only that, but there was not enough room for me to sit with my colleagues, so I had to sit on a different floor, in a different department. To say that I felt insecure would be an understatement. Bored, separated from my peers, with whom I wasn't terribly thrilled to begin with, I was beyond insecure; I was borderline catatonic.

Knowing what I know now, it is no mystery to me that everyone else appeared insecure to me. I had no other lens through which to view the world. But why was I so insecure? Because I was full of fear. As a result, I was completely disconnected from the life process. I felt dead, hopeless, unloved, abandoned, and punished. I was worried that I didn't have what it would take to succeed. I was the ultimate victim, and although it bothered me, I was jealous of anyone who seemed to be moving forward.

Sound familiar? I do not know a single person who has not felt this way to one degree or another at some point in life. Why is insecurity so pervasive? Because our deeply rooted belief that we are bodies and brains/minds has separated us from our source, from Spirit, from God. When we see ourselves as separate from our source, we cannot feel the energy of life within us, we do not trust that our needs will be met, and any time that we feel threatened, we feel insecure. And, unfortunately, we feel threatened most of the time.

It is a tragedy that the cornerstone of our civilization is fear. It is even more tragic that we prefer to listen to doomsayers and negative pundits, who are never lacking for evidence to justify our insecurities, than to muster the courage to think for ourselves and take the steps necessary to extricate ourselves from the existential trap we have set for ourselves.

Because we have surrendered our lives to fear, we feel that in order to be prepared for the worst, we must continually remind ourselves what pain feels like. Then we wonder why life has become a nightmare. But we are not simply bodies with brains/minds. We are living Souls, connected to all that is, was, and ever will be. Nightmares are illusions, not reality. All we need to do to escape from a nightmare is to simply *wake up*.

Let's check in with someone who did.

Beth, age forty-two, is a secretary to several account executives in an advertising agency. She returned to work one year ago because she needed to earn money to pay for her two high-school-age children's college education. Prior to her job raising her two children, Beth was the executive assistant to the president of a manufacturing company and was making a very good salary. Soon after she decided to reenter the workforce she found, much to her dismay, that her prior experience was considered outdated and that she lacked the computer skills necessary to succeed. She took classes at a local community college to learn the computer and the latest word processing programs and landed her current entry-level job after a three-month search.

"Even though my job as a secretary was not very challenging, I enjoyed going to work because I developed a very close friendship with Elaine, another secretary in the company who had returned to work a year before me after raising three children. Elaine and I had a lot in common and kept each other going when things got crazy. Three months ago, however, the situation changed dramatically when Elaine was promoted to the position of coordinator of secretarial services. Despite my best efforts, our relationship deteriorated as Elaine became more and more distant from the secretarial staff, started berating her former friends for minor infractions of the company code, and began hanging out with upper management. She appeared nervous and insecure and seemed to take her anxiety out on the secretaries.

"I hate to admit it, but I was jealous of Elaine's growing popularity with upper management. I began to realize just how dissatisfied I was with the way my career was going. I had always felt overqualified for the job and was frequently bored out of my mind, but now I felt that I was a victim of Elaine's good fortune and her resulting insecurity. I was feeling intensely depressed, and my hopelessness was affecting my husband and my kids. My husband suggested that I needed to confront the situation, figure out where my feelings were coming from, and most importantly, practice some of the spirituality that I had been studying. To be honest, it took several weeks for me to see that it was I who was filled with insecurity. Eventually I recognized that my current predicament was just the challenge I needed to confront and improve my work life. I also realized that I needed to reestablish honest communication with Elaine.

"I asked Elaine to lunch, explained how I was feeling, gave her some positive feedback about the things she was doing well, and gave her a few practical suggestions about how she could resolve her current relationship with the secretaries. She thanked me for reestablishing our friendship, apologized for taking out her insecurity on me, and suggested that I might be a great liaison with the secretaries since I had such good 'people skills.' I told her that I would love to help her out. Three months later, thanks to her relationship with upper management, Elaine successfully convinced the 'powers that be' that she needed a co-coordinator to help with day-to-day problem solving. I am happy to report that I am now the co-coordinator of secretarial services and feel more challenged in my job."

THE INSECURITY TRAP

In order to understand Beth's process of awakening and apply the method she used to our own lives, we need to get down and dirty with the issue of insecurity. The problem I have with most books on work is that they outline a plan for the reader to follow to improve his or her work situation without directly confronting what has caused the particular situation or problem. It is not possible to move forward in any area of our lives if we do not become accustomed to asking why we are in the predicament we are in before we tackle the issue of how to improve or eliminate it.

Let's be blunt. The vast majority of people on the planet, even the most seemingly strong and healthy, are insecure. We are insecure because we know that we are going to die. From the moment we realize that we are material beings with a finite life span, we become hostages to fear, insecurity, and anxiety.

Children at two years of age have not as yet realized that they will someday die. As a result, they are not afraid to test the limits of their abilities or to enthusiastically explore their environment. Because they have not developed a high degree of reasoning ability and do not as yet have decades of life experience or social and moral conditioning, they have not yet succumbed to fear. Unless their parents or caregivers are deeply troubled, every day of life is a grand adventure; every day is full of surprise and delight. Later something happens. They are severely reprimanded by an adult because they hurt themselves during one of their adventures. Their pet dies, or they watch as a close relative deteriorates due to a devastating illness. Eventually the realization dawns that the world is a dangerous place because all living creatures die. Thus begins children's initiation into the "I Hate Life Club."

A few years ago, I was shocked when I realized that my earliest conscious memory was of John F. Kennedy's assassination. My little sister and I were pulling our bag of blocks out of the closet while we were watching television. As a special news bulletin about the death of the president interrupted our program, my mother came running into the room. I remember my sister and I trying to make sense of the event as we tried to comfort our mother as she began to cry.

By the time I was eight years old, not only John Kennedy, but Robert Kennedy and Martin Luther King, Jr., had also been assassinated. In addition, my brain had been impressed with countless images of the horrors of the Vietnam War. These events and images profoundly affected me. Between the ages of ten and eleven, I suffered from severe insomnia. In retrospect, it is obvious to me that I didn't want to sleep because I was afraid I might die. Every night I focused my undivided attention on the same unanswerable questions: Could war break out here? If it did, would I survive? What if I died in a car accident? What if I got leukemia? What if . . . What if . . . What if . . .

I eventually overcame my insomnia, because, like a good soldier, I pushed my fears and anxieties out of my conscious awareness and into my unconscious mind. Existential terror no longer kept me up at night, but it didn't go away. It lurked behind the scenes, secretly directing my actions, holding me prisoner.

My story is not unique. Several summers ago, I was visiting my godson, who was then about five years old. As we were playing, he told me, out of the blue, that it was necessary to watch out for the bad men who could hurt you if you weren't careful. My godson has very attentive, well-adjusted, and loving parents. They live in a very nice suburban neighborhood and they are financially very secure. How did my little friend get so afraid? Turn on the television at any time of the day if you want to find the answer to that question.

Given that the level of violence has escalated in our society, it is hard not to believe, consciously or unconsciously, that we live in a dangerous universe and that death could come for us at any moment. Even the most well-adjusted people live in a constant state of low-grade fear, anxiety, and insecurity, whether they recognize it or not. Our need to protect ourselves is so strong that we are always on guard, judging the safety of every situation we encounter and the motives of every individual with whom we come in contact. We go out of our way to please anyone in a position of authority, especially parents and teachers, because we cannot go it alone. It is painful giving up our will, our individuality, and our vitality in exchange for a false sense of security, but we deeply believe that it is necessary for our survival.

We believe that our attachment to life is so tenuous that we cannot afford to make any mistakes. At first we avoid taking risks, and then after a while we simply accept that we cannot do what we want to do because everything is just too dangerous. We sacrifice our lives in order to stay alive. We prefer the safety of boredom to venturing forth into the jungle of the unknown. We are blind to the fact that because we have focused all of our mental energy on keeping our fear of death out of our conscious awareness, we are, for all intents and purposes, already dead.

But our Souls know better. Our higher self does not have to rely on belief, because it is nurtured and fueled by the energy of the universe, by Spirit, and has access to the wisdom of the ages. It knows that there is no death, because everything is energy, and energy can be neither created nor destroyed; it can only move and change. Our higher self understands that we are suffering due to our attachment to material reality. It wants us to surrender the illusion of death for the reality of everlasting life. And so it takes every opportunity it can to shake us up, knowing that, sooner or later, we will choose life over death.

CHANGE: THE ULTIMATE INSECURITY TRIGGER

Our Souls create changes in our lives to quicken our evolutionary process. Just when we think we've adjusted quite well to the role we've chosen to play, life throws us a curveball and forces our hand.

Beth's story is a perfect example. After spending many years as a successful full-time wife and mother, financial reasons forced her back into the workforce. To add insult to injury, she found that her previous work experience had become null and void. Whether Beth liked it or not, she was forced to reinvent herself.

Beth's story is not unusual. Many women returning to the workforce after raising children find out that the skills they developed and the successes they achieved prior to becoming full-time mothers are not considered valid in today's competitive marketplace. Many women like Beth must reinvent themselves if they want to return to the workplace. But it is not only women returning to the workforce who must reinvent themselves. In fact, many of us have already done so many times in the course of our work lives, and more of us will be forced to do so in order to survive and flourish in the ever-changing economic landscape.

Reinvention is not a bad thing; after all, adaptation is the key to evolution. But the process isn't easy, because when we are forced to change, adapt, or begin again at the bottom, we come face-to-face with our deepest and most powerful fears, insecurities, and anxieties, which can sabotage our best intentions if they are not recognized and transmuted.

When Beth returned to the workforce, she was starting all over again at the bottom. She was not very challenged by her work, but found meaning in her job through her friendship with her coworker, Elaine. Then, when Elaine was promoted, Beth's reality was severely shaken and a whole panorama of hidden emotions came rushing to the surface of her conscious mind. With this one change, Beth's world began to deteriorate, and insecurity and unhappiness were the end result. But, as we now know, these feelings were there all along, waiting in the shadows for the right moment to make themselves known.

WHOSE INSECURITY IS IT ANYWAY?

People usually see me as a strong, outgoing, secure individual, and for the most part I am. But most people outside my family do not know that I was an insomniac as a child. They don't know how long and hard I struggled with intense fear. Until ten years ago, I was afraid to pick up the phone, answer the door, or go to a party by myself. I couldn't take a bus because I was terrified of getting lost. There were years I spent more time crying than doing anything else. Why didn't anybody know? Because I was afraid to be weak. I was so ashamed of these feelings that I simply learned how to put on a good face for the world and how to hide my fears and resulting insecurities inside.

Beth had done the same thing. And because her relationship with Elaine was keeping these feelings at bay, she was deeply resentful when the relationship changed course. Because she was blind to how she was truly feeling about her work and her life on the deepest of levels, she could only project those insecurities onto Elaine. Now Beth could blame Elaine for her own unhappiness and take herself off the hook.

This is not to say that Elaine wasn't insecure or wasn't taking out her anxiety on Beth and the other secretaries. On a spiritual level, however, there is only one life Spirit. Beth would not have been able to recognize Elaine's insecurity and anxiety if she herself wasn't also insecure and anxious. This is a difficult concept to understand, given that we put so much stock in external reality. We seem to think that everything that happens on the external stage has nothing to do with us, that reality happens by accident, that we have no role in creating the situations we face. This is ludicrous. If we have no role in creating our reality, then why are we here? Are we the puppets of the gods? Are we merely victims of circumstance with no power whatsoever?

BRIDGING THE GAP BETWEEN EXTERNAL AND INTERNAL REALITY

I think that many of us resist acknowledging our own role in creating our reality because it is too painful to look at ourselves without the masks we wear to avoid pain and confrontation. Recently I began to question why I have always been an "insecurity magnet." Ever since I was a child, I have felt bombarded by needy and insecure people who were desperate for my friendship and approval. Many times over the course of my life I decided that enough was enough. But just as I would somehow manage to extricate myself from one needy, insecure relationship, another would magically appear in my life. I was completely blind to my own role in creating this horribly annoying pattern.

Recently an acquaintance attached herself to me like glue. If I was talking to someone else and she was around, she would interrupt the conversation and try to get me to focus my attention on her. Everywhere I went, there she was. It seemed as if her sole motivation was to get and keep my attention. She was driving me stark raving mad. I asked a good friend of mine who had witnessed some of the more obvious episodes what I should do. She said that I should figure out why I had attracted the situation to me. I felt like strangling her. I knew that she was perfectly right, but I couldn't help being offended by her insinuation that I had some role in creating the situation. I wanted to be a victim of circumstance. I didn't want to take responsibility. I went home and pouted.

When I couldn't pout any longer, an image of myself as a very small child came to me. I was so afraid and insecure. I needed my mother's undivided attention. I didn't want to be alone. Then I saw my little sister's face. She wasn't getting any attention. There was no time for her. Because I needed to be the most important thing in the whole world, my little sister had to suffer in silence. My needy, insecure acquaintance was me after all. I called my sister and apologized, and our relationship has improved as a result. Lately my acquaintance seems to be getting stronger and doesn't seem to require all of my time and attention. The question is: Did she change, or did I?

JEALOUSY

When we are insecure, our minds cannot tolerate those people who seem to be moving ahead. Because we have decided that we cannot do what we want to do, we feel inferior to those people who aren't stuck. Then we resent them and ultimately we are jealous of them. When Elaine was promoted, Beth felt abandoned and was jealous of Elaine's success. Most people would assume that Beth's reaction to her situation was very logical. But it is only logical if we give our minds total control over our actions. Because our minds are completely tethered to material reality, they cannot see the big picture, they cannot see beyond the boundaries of personal experience.

The mind derives its pleasure and happiness from external reality. It has been well trained in the art of comparing and contrasting, analyzing and critiquing. It doesn't accept life as it is; it judges every situation as either good or bad, right or wrong. It only wants to have its needs met, at any cost. When something of a positive nature happens for someone else, the mind fills with fear, is overwhelmed with feelings of inferiority, asserts its desire for power and domination, and responds with the powerfully negative emotions of jealousy and envy.

When we feel jealous or envious of someone else's success, we need to shift our attention to our Souls and take stock of what is happening on the internal level that is bringing such negative emotion to the surface.

Ever since I was a small child I loved music. I was a member of the school chorus and looked forward to rehearsals and performances. In fourth grade I was given the opportunity to begin studying an instrument. I chose the flute and quickly became very good at it. Some of my fondest memories of elementary school involved singing and playing my flute in the school band and orchestra. Then came junior high school. I was forced to choose between joining the chorus, the orchestra, or the band. I was torn because I loved singing as much as I loved playing the flute. I felt compelled to continue with the flute, however, because my parents had bought one for me, because I loved it so much. I felt they would be disappointed if I decided to give it up.

I continued to develop as a flute player and even became first chair in the flute section of my junior high school orchestra. In eighth grade the chorus put on a production of *Oliver!*, and as I sat watching the production, I felt tremendous longing welling up inside of me. I tried to push back my emotion, but I found that I was tremendously jealous of the girl who played the female lead. The next semester, I took a music appreciation class. One day the teacher, who was also the choral director, played the soundtrack of *Godspell* and asked the class to sing along. As the class ended, she came over to me and complimented me on my voice. I was happy with the compliment, but I was also upset. I desperately wanted to sing, but still felt compelled to continue with the flute because by this time my parents were paying for me to take private lessons. I continued my lessons for a few years, and before each and every lesson I couldn't understand why I was filled with horrible fear, dread, and nausea.

When I got to high school, my jealousy expanded as I met people who were involved in the choral music department. Because I was part of an honorary music society, thanks to my flute playing, I met some singers who were part of an elite female a cappella singing group. I envied them desperately, so much so that I couldn't bring myself to attend any of their concerts. By this time, I was no longer the best flute player in the orchestra. I was struggling to maintain my position as fifth chair. My skills were not improving because I was totally bored and disinterested. My heart was elsewhere, but I still couldn't acknowledge this simple fact to myself.

One day, during a flute lesson for which I was totally unprepared, my teacher stopped me as I tried for the hundredth time to play a particular passage. She turned to me and said, "Did you ever consider becoming a singer?" I almost fell on the floor. I felt like crying as I completely opened up to her about my secret desire to give up the flute and sing. After I finished pouring out my heart to her, she said, "Why don't we make this lesson your last?" I felt the heavens open up and I rushed home, told my parents I was going to pursue singing, put on every record I owned, and sang until I could sing no more. Surprisingly enough, my parents accepted my decision to change my musical direction without any discussion whatsoever.

That spring I auditioned for the elite female singing group, the object of my jealousy and my thwarted desire. Even though I had never sung for an audience before, I got in. After the audition, the choral director came over to me and said, "Where have you been all these years?" I didn't say anything but I should have told her that I had been in prison, the prison of fear.

The funniest part of all was that the next year I played one of the leading female roles in *Godspell*. My journey from death to life began with the realization that the opposite of jealousy is duty. And the greatest duty anyone ever has is to follow his or her heart's desire.

HEALING

Like Beth, in order to heal ourselves from the devastating effects of insecurity, we must (1) understand what causes insecurity to influence our lives; (2) understand that other people mirror our insecurity back to us to show us what we are unable to see in ourselves; (3) confront the faulty beliefs and negative emotions that are fueling its flames; and (4) take the steps necessary to transmute insecurity into opportunity.

We have already discussed at length Steps 1 through 3, but before we can move on to Step 4, we must move to an even higher level of understanding of the nature of reality. If there is no such thing as spiritual reality, and material reality is all that exists, if we are simply bodies with advanced brains/minds who are restricted by time and space, if death is indeed undeniably inevitable, then why would we even bother to seek solutions to our problems? Why wouldn't each and every one of us simply become an amoral sociopath? Why would we even strive to attain happiness, understanding, or peace? The answer is that we wouldn't.

If we weren't constantly evolving, if we weren't already aware of the truth on some level, we wouldn't feel compelled to seek any knowledge whatsoever. But we do seek knowledge. For the most part, we do not enjoy being unhappy and insecure for inordinate periods of time. Why is this? Because the Soul is the power behind the mind, and Spirit is the power behind the Soul. The more we become consciously aware of our spiritual nature, the more the mind's true nature is revealed. The mind is an illusion. Material reality is an illusion. We will evolve. Eventually our bodies, minds, and Souls will become one, and we will become agents of Spirit, of the Divine. We have no other choice. In fact, we are already there.

Several years ago, I succeeded in finding just the right job for a candidate named Richard. He was a diligent, hardworking, and personable young man who had a few years of experience under his belt and wanted very much to move into a management role. Within about six months, Richard was offered a supervisory position at another firm, and he jumped at the opportunity. After a few weeks at his new job, Richard called me to tell me that he was completely miserable and was feeling intensely insecure. It seems that one member of his staff was disregarding any assignments he gave to her, talking behind his back, and badmouthing him to anyone who would listen. On one occasion, she openly criticized him in a meeting with his staff. He was clearly distraught and wanted to know what he should do.

I told him that I thought the problem was clearly jealousy and that he should consider speaking to her about her feelings. He was not thrilled about having an open discussion with her, but said that he would try to engage her in dialogue. A few weeks later he called to give me an update on the situation. It seems that Richard's new colleague was about ten years older than he, had applied and interviewed for the supervisory position that Richard was hired to fill, and didn't find out that she didn't get the job until the day that Richard arrived. She was devastated and, feeling too insecure to confront the people who had really harmed her, she had taken her feelings out on Richard. Richard told her that he needed her expertise on the team, encouraged her to bury the hatchet, and asked her to help him build a topnotch staff. She thanked him for caring about her feelings and agreed to help him out.

It is clear that Richard did the right thing. By opening a channel of communication with his new colleague, he was also opening a channel of communication with the part of himself that was insecure. By confronting insecurity head-on, he eliminated its need to sabotage his positive, constructive efforts as a first-time supervisor. By showing understanding and compassion toward his new colleague, he was providing her with an opportunity to let go of her insecurity and join him in a common cause. Seen in this light, his new colleague was a gift, not a curse.

Beth did the same thing. She didn't fuel her insecurity by permitting herself the luxury of hating Elaine or gossiping behind her back. She was honest with Elaine about her feelings, but she didn't stop there. She gave Elaine positive reinforcement for the things she was doing well and offered suggestions about how to become even more successful. In the end Beth was rewarded for transmuting her boredom, jealousy, and insecurity, with the opportunity to join Elaine in the winner's circle.

Richard and Beth found the key to awakening from the nightmare of insecurity. Even though they may not have consciously realized that there are no people, places, situations, or things, because the only thing that really exists is energy or Spirit, they allowed their Souls, and not their minds, to direct their actions. In so doing, they took another step on their spiritual journey and got a taste of the peace, contentment, and success that is our right as spiritual beings.

EIGHT

MANAGING YOURSELF
AND OTHERS

At the end of the last chapter we met Richard, who felt that in order to progress in his career, he needed to move into a management role. I understand how he felt. After only one short year out of college I was determined to move up the career ladder. The only way that I saw to do this was to become a supervisor. In retrospect, it seems funny that I felt the need to move to a higher level after only one year on the job. I now see that there were both positive and negative aspects to my strong desire for more responsibility.

On the positive side, I had always been the kind of person who needed a challenge in order to get motivated. I always strived to be the best, the smartest, the most talented student, daughter, sister, friend, and so on. I never let up on myself, and on many levels my competitive nature paid off: I was smart, I was talented in many different areas, and I had a lot of friends.

There were also negative consequences, however. I couldn't

really say that I was happy. Because I was always focused on the next goal, on getting ahead, on taking on more and more responsibility just to prove I could handle it, I became a change junkie. I needed change in my life. As soon as I reached a goal, I felt the uncontrollable urge to move up, move forward, move ahead. It became impossible for me to just "be." I couldn't tolerate standing still. I would not allow myself to relax. I resented anything or anyone that threatened to hold me back. The compassionate, kindhearted side of my personality was always at war with the side that wanted recognition, acceptance, and, as hard as it is for me to admit, power.

Needless to say, I was not the prototype for the perfect supervisor. Yet I was promoted and was responsible for supervising a staff of about ten people. What is most remarkable is that I was the last person to be hired, the youngest member of the department, and the one with the least amount of experience. How did this happen? Very simply put, I campaigned for the job, and no one else did. I believed with all my heart that the job was rightfully mine. My desire was so strong that there was no way that Spirit could refuse my wish. The good news was that I had achieved yet another goal. The bad news was that I was totally unprepared to act as a leader.

As usual, my personal experience is not unique. Every day new supervisors and managers are appointed in the workplace who do not have the faintest idea how to proceed. As we all know, there is nothing worse than a bad supervisor or manager. But why are most people unprepared for management roles?

Deep within the human heart is the desire for power. When we see ourselves as bodies and minds without a connection to anything higher than material reality, this desire for power translates into futile attempts to manipulate external circumstances. At the beginning we simply try to control our environment, but when our efforts fail, instead of admitting defeat, we raise the ante and attempt to dominate it. We are so desperate to feel that we are in charge, that we cannot allow ourselves or anyone else to make any mistakes. We cannot tolerate surprises, so we plan, we organize, we push, we shove, we dictate. We do everything we can to make ourselves feel important, powerful, and strong. What better way could there be to feel important, powerful, and strong than to get paid to boss other people around?

The human being who comes to the realization that he or she is a living Soul knows that external reality is simply the reflection of internal reality, and is therefore an illusion. The Soul understands that it is futile to attempt to control or manipulate circumstances from the outside. The Soul knows that true power comes from its source, Spirit or God, which can only be found within. Only the individual who has acquired spiritual knowledge is truly capable of leading others. Only the individual who has dedicated his or her life to self-mastery is qualified to manage others. Only the individual who can motivate him- or herself is able to motivate others.

Angela, age forty-five, is divorced and the mother of three high-school- and college-age children. She is the manager of a fast-food restaurant in a not-so-affluent neighborhood of a major city. Most of Angela's employees are high school kids, including some unwed mothers and single fathers working to make money to help support themselves and their families. As a single mother, Angela can relate to the teenage kids who work for her. She empathizes with their situation and coordinates their work schedules around their school and family obligations.

"I find that if I show respect to my employees and show compassion for their personal situations, then I have an easier time managing and coordinating their responsibilities on the job. I don't see it as a crime against humanity, for example, if employees have to come in a little late or rearrange their schedule because they have to see their kid's teacher or take their mother to the doctor. I have to balance my work and family life, and so do they. I have few problems with my employees because I show a good example and am able to listen to what these kids are saying. I don't believe that work is drudgery. Every day is an opportunity to learn from my employees and to incorporate their suggestions into how I manage the restaurant. Most of these kids want to work hard and do a good job.

"I work on the assumption that I am here as a manager to help my employees evolve and to see that they have the potential to succeed. Our restaurant is a very popular hangout for local kids, and because of the positive spirit my employees have and the respect they show the customers, we have relatively few conflicts. I am a tough manager and do not tolerate laziness. Showing respect for people and instilling discipline have helped me, as well as my employees, to stay on track, and make my job as a manager very fulfilling."

Clearly Angela is the kind of manager that most employees would love to have. Her success as a leader was the result of a long process of self-discovery, however. Before we can truly understand the management process from a spiritual perspective, we first need to examine the basic requirements for leadership, including commitment to self-mastery; developing trust; and devotion to the path of love, compassion, and respect.

SELF-MASTERY

Sometimes what we think comes easily to another individual is in actuality the result of a lot of hard work. I know Angela well enough to know that her life has not always been sunshine and roses. She grew up as the youngest of three children in a family where there was never enough money to go around. Her father, whom she loved dearly, died when she was a little girl. Her brother, the one closest to her in age, was tragically killed in a car accident when she was just a teenager. Angela was left with a mother who could not snap back from the two tragedies, and an older brother who rejected her as a way to distance himself from his own feelings of loss.

Even though she was an excellent student, Angela's mother persuaded her not to go on to college. After graduation from high school, she got a job as a receptionist in a large corporation and soon after married her high school sweetheart. By the time she was twenty-five years old, Angela had three children, a husband who had been laid off from his blue-collar job, and a mother who had been diagnosed with cancer.

For most of her twenties, Angela was understandably depressed, but something within her would not allow her to sink into desperation. In her heart she knew that life could be better. In her heart she knew that she would find the way out. Then her mother died, and her husband left her for another woman. Angela was now all alone with her children and her anger. She knew that she had come to a crossroads in her life. She could harbor all her pain and anguish, or she could find a way to let it all go and move ahead with her life. Her heart, which never let her down, urged her to follow the latter course of action.

For three years, Angela was in therapy with a wonderful counselor who supported, comforted, and pushed her to first understand and then release her pain. As she released herself from the bondage of her experiences, she began to undergo a spiritual awakening. She found herself reading spiritually oriented books, attending meditation classes, and even found that she had the urge to attend church. Eventually Angela found the spiritual path that was right for her, and she dedicated herself to it, body, mind, and soul. By following her heart, she was led back to her real self, her Soul. Once she turned herself over to this higher power within her, she was led outside herself to spread her wisdom to other people.

When I first met Angela and heard her story, my mind didn't want to believe it. My thoughts went something like this: *What is this, a fairy tale? Is this woman deluded? So, Angela suffered a few hard knocks, got some therapy, read a few spiritual books, and went back to church. Who hasn't? She's still just an ordinary person. She doesn't have an MBA from Harvard. In fact, she doesn't even have a college degree. She doesn't have the time or the money to attend seminars on effective management. She couldn't care less about the latest motivational techniques. She doesn't read* Business Week *or* The Wall Street Journal. *How could she possibly be an effective manager and motivator? Let's get real. I need someone much more glamorous to look up to. I can't get excited by the story of a manager of a fast-food restaurant.*

While the mind might crave an Ivy League MBA and a glamorous lifestyle, the Soul desires the Truth. The Soul doesn't need to be convinced that Angela is anything but ordinary. The Soul knows that Angela is extraordinary because she has not only acknowledged her pain, but also transmuted it. The Soul recognizes that Angela is a successful manager simply because she is no longer ruled by the power of her mind. She knows who she is and where she's going.

TRUST

Some people spend their entire lives trying to find out who they are but never seem to get very far; many don't even bother to try; and still others decide to take it on faith that they are spiritual beings and go about acting as such until their faith is eventually transmuted into knowledge. Angela falls into the third category. This is another reason why she is extraordinary.

But every single human being has the same potential to become extraordinary. Everyone, regardless of personal circumstances, level of education, or financial position, has practically limitless opportunities for spiritual awakening. This is so because we all share one thing in common: pain and suffering. While suffering is the human condition, it is also the bridge to liberation.

As we have said before, the Soul is the operator behind the mind, behind the emotions, behind the suffering. The Soul uses pain to push, prod, and cajole the mind to look beyond itself, to recognize its source. Sometimes when pain pins us up against the wall of life, the mind goes into hiding for a split second, and we not only feel the power of Spirit behind the wall, but also we merge with it. Sometimes when we are too exhausted to fight pain any longer, we surrender. Too tired to care, we give up and allow ourselves to fall. Then when we come around, we realize much to our surprise that something caught us. Something cared for us when we were too weak to care for ourselves.

We become living Souls at the moment we are able to trust that the energy of life, Spirit, or God of which we are composed will take care of all our needs. Why is it that we have no difficulty trusting that our lungs will keep us breathing or our hearts will continue pumping our blood, but we cringe at the idea of trusting that we are Souls whose spiritual birthright is "Ask and ye shall receive"?

The simple answer is that we do not believe that all of our needs will be met because we are afraid of Spirit or God. We erroneously believe that Spirit or God is some mysterious entity or force outside ourselves that is just waiting for us to make a mistake so that it can punish us. When we believe in a vengeful God, it is impossible to trust that the life process has our best interests at heart. No matter how hard we try, we cannot love a God who requires that we worship him or her out of fear. We cannot love a God that demands unconditional surrender in return for pain and suffering.

But we have been fooled by fear. God is not outside of ourselves waiting to pass judgment on every mistake that we make. God or Spirit lives within us and doesn't care what we want, because it is incapable of judging our needs. God or Spirit generously gives us exactly what we want, whether we consciously know what we want or not.

Fortunately the only requirement for contacting and directing this divine essence is to trust, even for a moment, that it is there. Jack, the brother of a friend of mine, told me the following true story about himself that vividly illustrates the power of surrendering to the higher power within.

"Because of a substance abuse problem, I was no longer able to perform my duties on the job. Eventually, when things got pretty bad, my supervisor confronted me and gave me the choice of being fired or acknowledging my problem and entering a twenty-eight-day rehabilitation program. Although I didn't really think that I had a serious problem and I didn't trust that my supervisor had my best interests at heart, I agreed to enter the rehab program in order to get my employer off my back and save my job.

"I never believed that I could rely on or trust anyone other than myself. I always thought that my willpower, cleverness, and resourcefulness were the only tools I had to survive in the world. Due to my rigid and skeptical attitude, I wasn't making much progress in the rehab program. Now I can see that I was completely filled with anger and fear.

"On my last night at the rehab center, my lack of trust in others clearly manifested itself in reality. I learned that, although I was to be released at six o'clock the next morning, the hospital staff had not sent my suitcase, clothing, wallet, and money to my unit. Even though it was the hospital's mistake, I was left with no choice but to vacate my room in the early morning because another patient was moving in.

"I became enraged. *How do they expect me to get home without my things or any money? They're always telling me to turn my life over to a higher power. I'll turn it over all right. I'm not going to lift a finger. They screwed up. I'm not asking for help or calling anyone to come and get me and I'm certainly not going to borrow money from any of the losers here in rehab. It's up to God now.* The funny thing was that even though I was obviously asking my higher power for help out of bitterness and rage, I really did surrender. I had no choice. That evening, one by one, all of my problems were solved.

"First, the only friend I made at the rehab center volunteered to loan me his bag which had for no reason been delivered to his room. Then I found a twenty-dollar bill—just enough money to get me home—in the pocket of a shirt I hadn't worn since my first day in rehab. Next, two residents came to say good-bye and jokingly packed my bag for me. Finally, an old friend called from out of the blue to ask me if I wanted her to meet me at the train station in the morning. I'll never forget that experience. I didn't lift a finger, and yet everything was done for me. This was an incredibly powerful experience for me because I realized that all of my needs *are* being met all the time, whether I know it or not."

After reading this story you might be saying to yourself, *This is a wonderful story, but what does it have to do with management?* The answer is easy. If you want to be a good manager, you first have to trust the life process. You have to believe that all *your* needs will be fulfilled before you can try to meet anyone else's needs. By trusting the life process, you begin to trust yourself, your instincts, and your intuitions.

If you want to be able to lead, you first have to learn how to follow. So, who or what must you follow? You must follow your

Soul, which, despite the protestations of your mind and ego, is your true self—the self who is connected to eternity. The self who knows no suffering or pain. The self who knows what must be done in any situation, regardless of the circumstances. The self who will never let you down. The self who will never lead you astray.

As I said at the beginning of the chapter, the first time I was responsible for supervising a staff of people, I wasn't a great success. In retrospect, I can see that I wasn't ready for this level of responsibility because I didn't trust myself. My ego was so desperate to prove that I could handle power, so desirous of attention and respect, that I wouldn't have been able to hear a message from my Soul if I tried. I was so worried about making a mistake that I found it difficult to trust most of the members of my staff, or my own instincts for that matter. Eager to please my superiors, I over-managed most of my staff and catered to the ones who complained the loudest. After a few years the thrill of supervising wore off, and I found myself in a new job working for the boss from hell.

For years I wondered why I landed in such an unpleasant and emotionally draining situation. I refused to see the law of cause and effect in operation. I refused to make the connection between my actions as a supervisor and my subsequent life experience with supervisors and managers. Even though I never believed in chance, I somehow rationalized my subsequent negative experiences with managers, supervisors, and bosses as bad luck. But my Soul didn't judge my faulty thinking. It simply kept reflecting my lack of trust on the mirror of external reality to show me the senseless pain that results. My Soul knew that when the pain got to be too much, I would turn to it for help. I am thankful I did.

People, whether they ever become managers or supervisors or not, who do not trust the life process cannot trust themselves and are incapable of trusting others. Practically speaking, if you are unable to trust, you will always have to do the lion's share of the work yourself. You will never be able to let down your guard and find the peace you so desperately seek. If you cannot trust, you will not find happiness, nor will you succeed in achieving your heart's desire, no matter how hard you try. Without trust, you can make a good living, live in a big house, wear fancy clothes, and own an expensive car. But without trust there is no love. Without love no job is really worth doing, and no life is worth living.

LOVE, RESPECT, AND COMPASSION

Most of the problems that exist in the workplace today could be resolved by the unanimous application of the positive feelings of love, compassion, and respect. Obviously Angela realized this and allowed her emotions to flow from herself to her employees.

Let's begin with love, the most misunderstood of all the emotions. Because most people see themselves as bodies and minds, great injustices have been committed in the name of love. We commit crimes of passion, we engage in war, we justify our harsh words to our children, our spouses, and our colleagues, and we rationalize our opinions and beliefs all in the name of love. But this is not love, and we are not simply bodies with brains/minds.

We are Souls and as such are inextricably linked to Spirit, our source. When we catch even a glimpse of the glory of our true nature, we cannot help but see that love is the essence of Spirit, which drives and nourishes the living Soul and the entire universe. We cannot help but wake up to the fact that love is power, the only power.

To love is to act as a living Soul. To love is to accept life and participate in it without judging it. Love means to be in the world, but not of it. True love means to surrender ourselves to Spirit, every moment of every day, on or off the job.

Respect naturally flows from love. Since all beings are aspects of the one great life of Spirit, then every being is a reflection of the divine, and is therefore equally deserving of respect. Every person is a Soul who is performing an important and unique function in the universe, or he or she would not be here. Anyone who is unable to respect every other living being does not love or respect him or herself. Anyone who does not love or respect him or herself is totally incapable of leading others, regardless of his or her other qualifications.

With respect comes compassion. Because there is in truth only one life, the sufferings of one Soul are the sufferings of every Soul. And since there is only one life, then it is impossible to judge or condemn anyone without condemning yourself. Compassion means to show infinite love, respect, and forgiveness to all, regardless of the nature of the error or mistake made, regardless of the intent of the wrongdoer. The compassionate leader never wavers in his or her belief in the inherent goodness in life. The true leader strives to emulate the great spiritual masters— Lao Tzu, Krishna, Buddha, Moses, Jesus Christ, and Mohammed. The effective manager, like Angela, leads by example and practices what he or she preaches.

THE NOBLE EIGHT-FOLD PATH TO MANAGING AND MOTIVATING OTHERS

Now that we have examined the requirements for leadership, let's finally return to Angela's story. Once I overcame my mind's cynicism, I was convinced that Angela possessed the necessary qualifications to be an effective manager; but I must admit that I was having a difficult time figuring out her management strategy. Then one day as I was reading one of my favorite books on spirituality, I came across the Buddha's Noble Eight-Fold Path for Enlightenment. It dawned on me that whether she knew it or not, Angela, having attained mastery over herself, as well as having developed trust, love, respect, and compassion, was walking the Buddha's path. What exactly does this mean? I indulge the Buddha's patience as I present my interpretation of his Noble Eight-Fold Path as a modern management strategy.

1. Right Understanding

The first step on the path is to accept that we live in a universe governed by law. Probably the most important of all the universal laws is that of cause and effect, or the law of karma. The far-reaching and mind shattering implication of this law is that *nothing* happens by chance, that there is no such thing as luck or coincidence. We are 100 percent responsible for the circumstances in our lives and can change them at will. The cause is the same as the effect. As you sow, so shall you reap.

Therefore, on the management level, if you are currently a manager or supervisor, the staff you are responsible for motivating and managing is the staff that you have attracted to yourself. You are the cause, and your staff is the effect. If the majority of your staff is lazy or unmotivated, it's time to honestly examine these qualities within yourself and take the steps necessary to transmute them into their positive counterparts. If you want a happy, upbeat environment in which to work, you have to first become happy and upbeat. If you want to manage people who go above and beyond the call of duty, you must first do likewise.

There is no way around it. You have to give to life what you want out of it.

2. Right-Mindedness

Having acquired a full understanding of the law of cause and effect, a leader who takes the second step on the path knows that he or she is not an ego housed in a body, but is rather a living Soul. This leader knows the difference between illusion and reality and seeks guidance and wisdom from Spirit in the same way that a child turns to its mother for comfort and love. The person who chooses to take this step walks his or her talk and is a light that shows the way out of darkness. The individual who has mastered right-mindedness is not attached to outcomes and has no desire to acquire power in the material world. He or she doesn't postpone life, but rather embraces it. This manager or supervisor is a mentor to others, has one foot in the workplace and one foot in heaven, and knows that anything worth achieving can be achieved. Because he or she believes it and can prove it, so do the members of his or her staff.

3. Right Speech

When we understand that we are spiritual creatures who have been given the ultimate freedom to choose the circumstances of our lives, we can naturally take the third step on the path by committing ourselves to speaking the truth. A manager who has risen to this level has no desire to take credit for something that someone on his or her staff did, nor does such a manager have any problem being honest with his or her staff members, superiors, or with him- or herself. To give credit where credit is due and to offer constructive criticism when appropriate is the mark of an evolved Soul because it implies true understanding of self-lessness and devotion to a higher master—the Spirit within.

4. Right Action

The manager who can gently speak the truth in any situation is ready to take the fourth step on the path. According to the Buddha, right action is any action that does not bring harm to any living creature. Therefore, right action is motivated by compassion, empathy, understanding, and love. Right action means sticking to the high road, avoiding office politics, gossip, and other useless and potentially harmful activities.

Right action does not mean that a manager should not set reasonable standards of behavior or expect a certain level of performance from his or her staff members. On the contrary, an effective manager, like a parent who is responsible for the welfare of his or her children, must sometimes act in a so-called negative manner in order to bring about a positive outcome. For example, if a staff member consistently does not meet the manager's performance standards and has been counseled on numerous occasions regarding how to meet these standards, right action might imply letting such an employee go. An evolved leader knows that spirituality is not a synonym for passivity.

5. Right Livelihood

The fifth step on the path is an admonition to make sure that the work that you are doing is valuable and life enhancing. Do you enjoy the work you are doing? Are you using your unique gifts and talents in service to the world and humanity? Are you doing what you want with your life? If not, it is highly probable that you are not an effective manager. It is impossible to create a successful staff if you are unhappy with your work. To be a real leader, you must be able to commit yourself—body, mind, and Soul—to the path you have chosen. If you cannot, you are not on the right path.

6. Right Endeavor

The sixth step on the path is to always fix your attention on the big picture by constantly reminding yourself that you and all the members of your staff are on the same evolutionary journey to know Spirit or God. Right endeavor means that you move through life as a living Soul, showing support, acceptance, love, and mercy to all those who need it, resisting the temptation to judge the actions of others, and never hindering your own or anyone else's progress on the spiritual path.

7. Right Recollection

The seventh step on the path is to think before you act. The leader who is dedicated to performing only right action has the power to review the past in order to make appropriate decisions in the present. If you find your mind filled with the negative emotion of anger, for example, you have the ability to review your past and isolate a time when you allowed yourself to freely express this emotion in order to see the negative consequences that came as a result. This review helps you to consciously choose a different reaction, such as patience, to express in the present, thereby transmuting the potential for a negative outcome into the reality of a positive one.

8. Right Concentration

The eighth step implies the ability and willingness to focus your energy on the real world of Spirit, rather than on the illusion of material reality. Knowing that Spirit will provide you with all that you need and want, you are indifferent to external things and are able to give freely, generously, and lovingly to all who depend on you for guidance and leadership. Because you only deal with the spiritual essence of any individual at any time, and due to your ability to concentrate your attention like a laser, you have the power to manifest the best possible circumstances for all involved in every situation.

Taking the First Step

Given the lofty requirements for leadership and the commitment required to walk the Noble Eight-Fold Path outlined above, it is no wonder that the number of effective managers and great leaders is so low. Does this mean, however, that we should not even try to develop these qualities in ourselves because they seem so difficult to attain? And how about those individuals who are already in management roles? Should they throw in the towel and admit that they do not have what it takes to lead? Of course not. Every breakthrough—spiritual or otherwise—begins with the first step, and every first step is difficult and painful. But if we desire happiness, if we desire any amount of liberation from the mundane, then we must put one foot in front of the other. We must allow ourselves to fall flat on our faces day after day until, like an infant, we learn how to walk. We can't allow ourselves to be so afraid of failure that we don't allow ourselves the opportunity to succeed.

Imagine the revolution that would occur in the world if more people in the workplace, at home, in the schools, and in government committed themselves to walking the spiritual path. What would happen if more people wanted to lead out of a desire to express love, respect, and compassion than as a means to accumulate power and prestige? Take the first step and find out.

NINE

PLAY YOUR PART

In the last three chapters we have tackled the most difficult of all the spiritual principles: the illusion of other people. As we have said many times, on the most basic of levels the only thing that really exists is energy or Spirit. The material or external plane of existence is nothing more than a reflection of the spiritual or internal world of the individual. Practically speaking, this means that you can only see the world as you are, not how it is. Put another way, the flaws and failings we see in other people are simply our own flaws and failings projected onto the screen of external reality. Therefore, we are not separate from the people, places, situations, or things we observe; we are actively participating in creating them.

I must admit that this concept was the most difficult for me to accept because I enjoyed seeing myself as separate from other people. I was very proud of my own uniqueness and was arrogant and self-righteous enough to believe that the negative traits I found so objectionable in other people were somehow justifiable and appropriate when I was expressing them. I have a sneaking suspicion that down deep most people feel exactly the same way.

Denying the reality of life does not change it, however. If we want to be happy and successful, we must replace our self-righteousness and arrogance with understanding and compassion. We must have the courage to look in the mirror of external reality and see what we have allowed ourselves to become. We must force ourselves to look at the horrible face of our creation and see the flaws, failings, and negative traits we have tried so hard not to recognize as our own. Then we must summon the strength to forgive ourselves for our ignorance and ask Spirit to show us the way home.

Shakespeare said that all the world's a stage, and he was right. Everything that exists in the material world is nothing more than energy or Spirit temporarily frozen into matter. But matter, unlike Spirit or energy, which is omnipresent, omniscient, and omnipowerful, is not eternal. It is transient and fleeting, just like the scenery used in a theatrical production. Unlike other forms of matter, however, we humans are Souls, self-conscious spiritual beings housed in material bodies. We are actors playing our parts in the illusory drama of material reality, but unlike theatrical characters whose lines always remain the same in every production, our parts are constantly evolving, and our lines are always changing. And, best of all, because we are Souls, we are not only actors, but also the directors, producers, and scriptwriters of our own lives.

THE DIRECTOR

In movies, television, and theater, the director is the person entrusted with complete artistic control over the production, the person whose job it is to transform an idea or vision into a television show, or play. Likewise, we are the directors of our own lives and as such have complete responsibility for and control over the quality of our reality. We are not the puppets of the gods. We are not controlled by some external force whose job is to manipulate us like the pieces on a chessboard. The truth is that we are in charge, whether we like it or not. But the question is: What aspect of ourselves is running the show, our minds or our Souls?

Until we recognize our role as directors and see that we are responsible for the quality of our own lives, we allow our minds to control our actions, and before long we become the slaves of fear, pain, and suffering. But when the pain and suffering eventually get to be too much and the weight of our minds becomes unbearable, our desire for peace and happiness leads us to investigate whether there might not be a better way to live, and sooner or later we find ourselves on the spiritual path.

Once on the path we are given a choice. We can renounce our former fearful and painful lives and the aspect of our personality that brought us to that unhappy state, and embrace the unknown country of our Soul, our higher nature, our connection to the divine—or we can return to our old life and pick up where we left off. Let us find the courage to move from the known to the unknown, to replace fear with faith, to overcome the illusion of physical death by embracing the everlasting life of Spirit. We can begin by allowing ourselves to turn the control of our lives over to the spiritual aspect of our nature, to our Souls.

Step 1: Surrender

Sit quietly for a few moments. Relax your body and mind until you feel totally at peace. Immerse yourself in this feeling for as long as you can. Everything is perfect. Your life is perfect. You are perfectly healthy—physically, mentally, and spiritually. You are surrounded by the light of faith and love. Now imagine yourself in a beautiful natural setting. You could be at the beach, in the mountains, by a lake—anywhere where you feel comfortable and peaceful. You are completely relaxed and happy and are not surprised when you notice that someone is walking toward you. You instantly recognize that this person walking toward you is your Soul, your divine self. Immediately you are filled with joy. Your Soul looks exactly like you. It is you. Your Soul is beautiful. It radiates faith, hope, love, duty, compassion, kindness, and patience. Now your Soul is only a few feet away from you. It holds out its arms, and you walk toward it and embrace it. You feel the warmth of your Soul penetrating your body and mind. The warmth is melting away all of your fear, all of your pain. You are completely filled with love. Softly you ask your Soul to take control of your life, to lead you and guide you on the path to complete understanding. Your Soul joyfully agrees to be your guide and to direct your actions. See yourself merging with your Soul. You and your Soul are now one.

THE PRODUCER

Even though the director is responsible for the overall vision and direction of a production, he or she will not get far if there is not a competent producer on board to handle the day-to-day issues and difficulties that arise. With respect to our own lives, we need not look any further than our Souls to take on the responsibilities of the producer. Our Souls have a limitless capacity for work and will gladly handle not only the overall direction of our lives, but will resolve any problem that threatens to keep us from reaching our goals.

By now we are well aware that it is our thoughts that create our reality. Therefore, the problems we are faced with on a daily basis are the result of faulty or negative thinking. Because our minds have been controlling our thoughts up until now, we have become accustomed to focusing most of our attention either on reliving painful memories from the past or anticipating negative situations that may arise in the future. But if we are sincere in our desire to have our Souls act as the producers of our lives, if we want to live happy, successful, and peaceful lives, we have to release the painful and traumatic memories that the mind uses to hold us prisoner. While we must be aware that the mind will not give up control easily, let us forge ahead confidently, knowing that even though the Soul might not win every battle, it will certainly win the war.

Step 2: Clean-up

1. On a piece of paper, write down every horrible, painful, or embarrassing experience you can pull up from your memory. (Or you can record yourself recounting these experiences into a tape recorder.) Include any wrongs committed against you by other people, as well as wrongs you have committed. Don't be shy; no one is ever going to see your answers to this exercise. Be dramatic. Make sure to include all the gory details: how the situation occurred, how you felt, how you perceived other people felt, etc. Don't rush yourself with this exercise. As you put your memories down on paper, see them leaving your mind and consciousness. The more you write, the lighter you become.

2. If you feel so inclined, light a candle, burn some incense, or put on some music to get you in the mood to let go of these memories from the past. When you feel ready, burn or tear up the paper on which your memories are written. Repeat the

following phrase out loud to yourself several times as you release the past:

> "As I let go of these negative memories from my past, I
> release any power they may have over me. I ask that when
> my attention turns toward these memories or toward any
> negative thought or emotion, my Soul gently guides me
> back to the life-affirming power of the positive."

3. Begin to incorporate this procedure into your daily life. Practice releasing negative memories as they come into your conscious awareness. Don't suppress the negative memories, just
let them go. Every so often during the day, notice what you
are thinking about. If you find that you are focused on a negative memory, bring your attention back to the present moment and repeat the phrase above several times. Alternatively,
focus all your attention on the negative memory and, using
your imagination, mentally transform the negative aspects of
the memory into positive images. If you are remembering a
time when someone was screaming at you, for example, see
the person speaking loving words to you in a soft and gentle
manner. It takes practice to control your thoughts, but it is
well worth the effort. As you become the master of your
thoughts, your Soul responds by producing a more beautiful
life for you.

THE SCRIPTWRITER

Just as our Souls are perfectly suited to be the directors and producers of our lives, they are equally well suited to be the scriptwriters. In material reality, the role of a scriptwriter or
playwright is to develop a cohesive, logical, and entertaining plot,
and characters to move the plot forward. Since the focus of the

next section of the book is how to develop a new script for your life, we will concern ourselves here and now with character development.

When we give our Souls the job of scriptwriter, we have the power to eliminate the negative and destructive characters from our lives and replace them with positive and supportive ones. But since the other people in our lives are only reflecting ourselves back to us, if we want to make changes in the casting of our script we have to be willing to focus our energies on changing those negative aspects of ourselves that are attracting those unpleasant characters into our lives. The following exercise is designed to help you to recast your script by learning how to transmute negative energy into positive energy.

Step 3: Transmutation

Divide a large legal-size piece of paper into eight separate columns and fill it in as follows:

1. In the first column, make a list of the coworkers (and bosses) from all your jobs (past and present) you would consider negative or with whom you have experienced difficulty.

2. In the next column, list any family members, if any, who remind you of each of these individuals.

3. In the third column, describe the negative qualities or the negative behavior exhibited by each of these individuals.

4. In the fourth column, determine which of the following sums up the behavior of each of these individuals: fear, greed, worry, anger, jealousy, criticism, or hatred.

5. In the fifth column, write down examples of how you exhibit similar negative qualities, behavior, and emotions.

6. In the sixth column, list the positive characteristic that is the opposite of the primary negative quality you identified in column four: fear/faith, greed/kindness, worry/hope, anger/patience, jealousy/duty, criticism/compassion, hatred/love.

7. In column seven, list recent situations from your life when you expressed these positive emotions.

8. In column eight, describe how you could express these positive emotions when dealing with the difficult or negative characters in your life.

THE ACTOR

Within the world of film, television, and theater, the actor's job is to take direction from the director, have his or her needs met by the producer, and read the lines written by the scriptwriter. On the most basic of levels, therefore, the actor is simply the vehicle through which someone else's vision is expressed and interpreted. We are all actors on the stage of life. When we allow other people to tell us how to live our lives, or when we give over our control to our minds, we are not expressing ourselves as we really are, Souls with a divine heritage and birthright. As a result, we are second-rate actors because our expression of life is hollow, shallow, and negative.

But once we begin to walk the spiritual path, something clicks within us and we get a taste of what it feels like to express joy and love. Intoxicated by the possibility that life could be free of pain, we leap into the void and vow to allow our Souls to act as the director, producer, and scriptwriter of our lives. After much practice and tireless effort, our Souls take over and our bodies and minds become the perfect vehicle through which Spirit can express itself.

Step 4: Relaxation

In order for our bodies to freely express Spirit, they must be relaxed. The following relaxation technique is fast and effective.

1. Sit in a straight-backed chair or stand, if necessary.

2. Close your eyes and breathe in slowly through your nose and out through your mouth several times until you feel calm and peaceful.

3. Focus your attention on the various parts of your body and gently move them around until they are completely free of tension. Start with your toes, move on to your feet, ankles, calves, knees, thighs, lower back, stomach, upper back, chest, arms, shoulders, neck, and face.

4. A few times per day, stop what you are doing and notice if any areas of your body appear tense. If so, take a few deep, slow breaths and then gently move these areas around until they are relaxed.

Step 5: Staying in Character

Some days it's difficult to think, talk, and act as a Soul. The following three exercises can help you to access your Soul, to stay in character during times of stress or crisis, or any time that you may feel that you have lost the way.

➤ *Soul Workout to Alleviate Frustration or Mental Confusion*
  Find a neutral place outside your normal work environment and sit in a chair, or if necessary stand. Close your eyes. Breathe in slowly through your nose and out through your mouth several times until you feel calm and peaceful. Isolate

any areas of your body that feel tense and gently move them around until they are relaxed. Repeat the phrase "Spirit, work through me to resolve this situation in the best possible manner for all involved," slowly, at least five times. Open your eyes when you feel ready. Take your time readjusting to your environment.

➤ *Soul Workout to Resolve Conflicts or Difficult Situations*
Find a neutral place outside your normal work environment and sit in a chair or, if necessary, stand. Close your eyes. Breathe in slowly through your nose and out through your mouth several times, until you feel calm and peaceful. Isolate any areas of your body that feel tense and gently move them around until they are relaxed. Now imagine yourself in a beautiful natural setting. You could be at the beach, in the mountains, by a lake—anywhere where you feel safe, comfortable, and peaceful. Recreate your peaceful place sensorially and allow yourself to feel as if you are there. If you are at the beach, for example, how would it smell? How would the sun feel on your face, your neck, your legs? How would the sand feel against your back or under your feet? What would the water feel like on your fingers, on your legs, in your mouth? Allow yourself to become completely immersed in the sensation of actually being at the beach. When you have completely surrendered to this feeling, allow the person or the situation that is causing you distress to appear at the beach. Invite the person to sit down next to you on the sand, or invite the situation causing you difficulty to unfold before you. Imagine how you would respond to the person or the situation from your centered, peaceful self. Open your eyes and slowly readjust to your environment.

➤ *Soul Workout to Reconnect with Your Spiritual Essence*
Find a neutral place outside your normal work environment and sit in a chair or, if necessary, stand. Close your eyes.

Breathe in slowly through your nose and out through your mouth several times until you feel calm and peaceful. Isolate any areas of your body that feel tense and gently move them around until they are relaxed. All of our memories are recorded in our muscles and in our cells and can be accessed when we are in a relaxed and peaceful state. Imagine a scene from your life when you freely and spontaneously expressed positive emotion. Allow yourself to feel completely what you experienced at that moment. How did it feel to show compassion, love, patience, hope, faith, duty, and kindness? If there was another person or other people there, how did they respond to you, your words, your actions? When you feel your entire mind and body immersed in this feeling, take your time and imagine yourself handling the situation or dilemma you are now confronted with in the external world. Open your eyes when you are ready. Slowly begin to readjust to your environment.

PART FOUR

YOU REAP WHAT
YOU SOW

FIGHT BACK

Lost among the shadows
Pinned between two clouds
It's hard to see the ocean
When it's raining up above
Balanced on the edge of time
Life proceeds without a sound
Always running toward the dawn
It takes the night to slow the storm
Forgetting pain is not the goal
When you travel fast you cannot hold
The feel of the moment
The depth of the soul
Stand up/Fight back
Refuse to give up what you know is right
It's your duty to be happy
It's your destiny to be free
You cannot fight the shadows
You can't destroy the clouds
The ocean will exist forever
The rain will always be
Stand up/Fight back
Never underestimate what you cannot see
It's our duty to be happy
It's our destiny to be free

—TAMI COYNE

TEN

ADVANCING WITHIN THE RANKS

We have covered a lot of territory so far on our spiritual quest. But before we jump into this next section of the book, which deals with the specifics of manifesting success in our lives, let's take a few moments to review the highlights of our journey so far.

The spiritual teachings presented in this book can be categorized into five principles: (1) Divine Truth; (2) Divine Heritage; (3) Divine Gifts; (4) Divine Law; and (5) Divine Birthright. The Divine Truth is the One Life Principle that states that because everything in the material universe is made up of energy—which is synonymous with Spirit or God—then Spirit or God is all that exists. There are no people, places, situations, or things. There is only one life essence, which expresses itself through different forms.

As humans, our relationship to the One Life, to the life essence, is unique because we are self-conscious and, as a consequence, are able to reason and choose. Our Divine Heritage is that we are Souls, not advanced clumps of matter who just happen to be able to think inwardly. When our reason allows us to see that because energy, God, or Spirit is all that exists, then we must be divine expressions of the One Life, we can choose to wrestle ourselves free from the domination of our minds. In so doing, we become living Souls, conscious expressions of divinity.

As living Souls, we are endowed with two divine gifts: right thinking and right action. Right thinking means the ability to transmute, at will, the negative mental elements of fear, greed, worry, anger, jealousy, criticism, and hatred into the positive spiritual elements of faith, kindness, hope, patience, duty, compassion, and love. Right action is any action that is inspired by the positive characteristics of the Soul, which assists the life process to unfold. In other words, any action that serves life is right action.

When we wake up to the fact that we are Souls, we become aware that the entire universe is governed by Divine Law, paramount of which is the law of karma, the law of cause and effect. When we understand the simple yet powerfully liberating truth of this Divine Law—that the cause is the same as the effect, than as Souls what we sow is what we reap, that we are the cause and our life is the effect—we can come to no other conclusion than we are 100 percent responsible for the quality of our lives. And with that realization comes the power to change any negative into a positive by first changing ourselves.

So far we have dealt with these first four spiritual principles in great depth as they apply to the workplace. It is now time to understand and claim the rewards of the fifth spiritual principle, our Divine Birthright, which is "Ask and ye shall receive." Now is the time to give ourselves permission to claim what is already rightfully ours: success, love, peace, happiness. Now is the time to take action to get what we want. We are expressions of divinity. Maybe we should act accordingly.

Evan, age twenty-eight, is married with a small child. He has a high school diploma and some additional computer training. After he had worked for several years in the photocopy/duplication department of a bank, for a woman who infused everything she touched with positive energy, his boss announced that she was retiring. Before leaving the bank, however, she pulled Evan aside and encouraged him to apply for an administrative assistant position that had opened up in the legal department.

Even though Evan was disappointed that his boss was retiring, he realized that it was time to move along with his career. His wife had just had a baby, and the new job came with a slightly higher salary, which Evan knew would come in handy. Because of his good reputation, and thanks to the recommendation of his former boss, he got the job.

"I had been working as an administrative assistant for about six months and was really enjoying my new position when my new supervisor decided to leave the company. Many of my colleagues were filled with anxiety about the prospect of a new supervisor and tried to get me to panic, too. But I realized that it would be stupid to look for a new job just when I was learning so much and enjoying my new responsibilities. Although it wasn't easy, I decided to have faith that the new supervisor would turn out to be a good person and would help me to grow. Of course, my coworkers had problems with Eileen, the new boss, because they expected to have difficulty. I, however, had a great time working with her.

"Shortly after she arrived, I made an appointment to see Eileen. I explained that I had taken some computer courses a few years earlier and was interested in developing my skills in that area. I also told her that I noticed that there were some departmental reports that were generated manually which I felt could be easily automated. I volunteered to do a little work in my downtime to develop a prototype of one of the computerized reports. Eileen was clearly happy with our meeting and told me to go ahead with my plan.

"Within a month, I was responsible for automating all departmental reports, and six months later, after the new report system was completely in place, I told Eileen that I was ready for more responsibility (and more money, too). Shortly thereafter, I was promoted to a supervisory position, which was unusual in my department because I didn't have a college degree. I was also earning significantly more than what I was earning when I began working in the legal department. With the extra money, I was able to relocate my family to a better neighborhood and am considering pursuing a college degree.

"I have always believed that the only way to get ahead is not to fall prey to the anxieties and worries of those around you. If you believe that good things can happen, take responsibility for yourself and your work, and take positive action to get things done, they will happen."

LAYING THE GROUNDWORK

Although it may seem old-fashioned or a cliché, we must first plant the seeds of our desires and allow them to grow before we can harvest the crop. Evan's success didn't come about overnight. He didn't wake up one morning to discover that he had a new job and was making more money than the day before. Over the course of time, he planted the seeds of success and nurtured them with his thoughts and his actions. He was promoted to the position of administrative assistant because he was already successful. He had developed a good reputation over several years as a member of the photocopy/duplication department. He showed up on time. He was responsible and pleasant. He did a good job. He saw his boss as a mentor and accepted any constructive criticism she gave him. He worked for his promotion. But not in the way that most people work.

In our present age, work is seen as negative because it implies effort and deferred gratification. For many of us, work is like exercise; if you don't feel the pain, you won't get the gain. Because we have been programmed to believe that work is supposed to be painful, Evan's story does not seem that exciting to us. He didn't suffer enough. He didn't plot or scheme to get ahead. He didn't even complain. In fact, he even seemed to enjoy the *process* of advancing as much as he enjoyed achieving his goal. His story is not dramatic enough to hold our attention. It would never get made into a movie of the week.

But the lack of drama in Evan's story is exactly the point. When we take a closer look, we can see that his story is much more than a nice tale about an average person who moved up a few notches on the corporate ladder. It is really a fable about how the Soul should proceed as it advances along the spiritual road to enlightenment.

OVERCOMING MENTAL PROGRAMMING

Unlike Evan, most of us don't think we can get ahead, due to reasons that are beyond our control. We don't have enough education. We're the wrong sex, race, or class. We're too fat, too thin, too old, or too young to succeed. We're just not good enough. With that kind of thinking, it's no wonder we're barely getting by.

This attitude is well and good if your goal in life is to be miserable and unhappy. But if you are harboring any secret hope that life is more than pain and suffering, it is now time to muster up the courage to say good-bye to those beliefs that are holding you back from living a better life. If you truly want to make your secret hope a reality, the first step is to recognize that the only thing standing in your way of achieving what you want out of life is you. There are no external forces holding you back. You are in charge. You are the master of your own destiny.

I learned this most important of lessons one day at work. As part of my job as a placement counselor for a post-college paralegal training program, I conducted individualized interview preparation sessions with entry-level paralegals for whom I was also responsible for finding jobs in the New York area. One day I had a very difficult schedule and was conducting sessions back-to-back for several hours without a break. After a particularly difficult prep session, I was relieved that my next appointment was with Jean, a very attractive recent college graduate from a highly respected university. Jean looked so professional and put together as she walked into my office that I was convinced our meeting would only be a formality. How wrong I was.

Jean had tremendous difficulty answering even the most simple of interview questions. She stumbled over her words and seemed on the verge of tears every time I offered some constructive criticism about how she might improve her interviewing style. When I finally realized I wasn't getting very far, I pulled out Jean's file, which I hadn't had time to review before our appointment, and quickly scanned it to see if there was some obvious reason for Jean's unbelievably bad self-presentation. Before I could find anything, Jean blurted out, "I didn't do very well in college. In fact, I just barely graduated. I didn't like the school. My parents got a divorce during my freshman year. I just couldn't get motivated. I don't think anyone is going to want to hire me with my grade point average."

After she finished, I looked at her undergraduate record. It was pretty bad. But then I noticed that she was in the very top of her paralegal training class, and she had taken the most difficult course of study. Just then, my next appointment was at the door. I didn't have any more time for Jean, and she desperately needed help. Suddenly I had an inspiration. I turned to Jean and said, "I know that you are a bright woman and I know that you can get a job. I want you to come back in an hour, during my lunch break, and we'll do this again. When you leave here, go someplace quiet where you won't be distracted. Relax yourself and then imagine that you graduated from Harvard University with a four point zero average. Then I want you to practice answering those interview questions we just went over. Okay?" She agreed.

An hour later, Jean was at my door. She had a huge smile on her face. She sat down and answered my questions like an old pro. I told her that I knew that I would only be able to arrange a single interview for her because I had only one client, a prestigious firm, that never asked me about an applicant's college grades. I told her that while many of her other classmates would have several opportunities to interview, she would only get one shot. She said she understood.

Jean got the job. In fact, the firm made her an offer on the spot which, of course, she accepted. Jean's story still astounds me. I have never met anyone who was so willing to let go of her old mental programming in order to succeed. I have never met anyone who was able to do it so fast. Simply by imagining that she was a winner turned her into one. Jean proved to me without a doubt that we are who we think we are, and that it is possible to reinvent ourselves at will.

Another applicant, however, taught me that we only receive from life what we expect to receive. While at this same job, I also handled the placement of experienced paralegals in jobs in the New York area. One day a man named Bob called me on the phone to make an appointment to meet me. When I asked if he could send me his résumé in advance so I could determine whether or not I would be able to help him, he replied that he was in the process of updating it and asked if he could bring it with him when we met. He sounded great over the phone, so I agreed.

When Bob walked into my office, I knew why he didn't want me to see his résumé in advance of our meeting. He was about sixty years old and wanted to leave his current job because it wasn't challenging enough. He was a great guy and had a great background, but I didn't think I'd have an easy time finding him a job because of his age. I told him about my concern, and when I finished, he smiled and said he understood. But before he left my office he told me, "I know there is a job out there for me. Just because I'm sixty doesn't mean that I should stay in a job that isn't challenging." Humbled, I agreed with him and sent his résumé to some clients who I thought might be interested in his background.

All the clients, except one, didn't even want to interview Bob. But the one who did want to meet with him just happened to be looking for someone very seasoned to work with some difficult clients. They didn't care in the least that Bob was sixty. My client loved Bob, and Bob loved the job. Current conventional wisdom dictates that it is nearly impossible to find a job if you are over fifty-five. Bob didn't care what other people, including me, thought was possible or impossible for him to achieve. He expected life to provide him with a challenging job, and it did. He asked and he received.

RISKING SUCCESS

My chiropractor and metaphysics teacher, Dr. Alfred Kayata, said something the other day that really impressed me. He said, "The current motivational phrase 'Don't be afraid to fail' should be replaced with the phrase 'Don't be afraid to succeed.'" After I gave it some thought, I realized he was absolutely right. It is ridiculous that even when we talk about success we phrase it in terms of failure. The truth is if we want to succeed, we should focus our entire attention on success. And, when thoughts of failure enter our conscious awareness, we should gently wash them away with positive images of the successful life we want to live.

Evan was not afraid to succeed. He was simply waiting for the right opportunity to arise. When the seeds of success he had sown were ready to harvest, his boss relayed the message to him from Spirit that it was now time to move forward to take on a new challenge. With the support and encouragement of his boss, and thanks to his great reputation within the bank, he got a job in the legal department and received a raise.

When we decide to risk being successful, we must first culti-vate the positive spiritual characteristic of patience. The bigger the risk, the more patience that is required. Since 1987, when a friend asked me to write an article on the paralegal field for a newsletter she had started, I wanted to become a professional writer. But I realized that this was not a short-term goal. It took ten years for my goal to materialize because there were many small steps that I needed to take to prepare myself for this new career. Likewise, if we want to be successful or advance in our careers or in any other aspect of our lives, we have to be prepared to do what is required of us at every stage of the game until the right moment for action appears.

It is no secret that the people who get ahead are patient, con-fident, do their jobs well, go above and beyond the call of duty, have a "can-do" attitude, and are positive and upbeat. These peo-ple see life as an adventure, not as a struggle. They do not panic at the first sign of trouble. You will not find them whining and complaining about how bad things are, how poorly they are treated, or how much more money they deserve to make. Let's face it, if you want to get ahead, you have to do more than dress for success; you have to think, talk, and act successful. Then, when the time is right, you will find yourself advancing a little further along the highway of life.

THE HONEYMOON PERIOD

After Evan got promoted to the position of administrative assistant in the legal department, he underwent what I like to call the honeymoon period. After the stress of the initial transition period went away and Evan got the hang of the new job, everything went swimmingly. He found that he liked his new colleagues, his work was challenging, and he was glad that he left his old department. In many ways, Evan was reborn and had even higher hopes for his future as a result of his having risked advancing in his career.

A honeymoon period also occurs in the internal life of the Soul after we have taken a few initial steps on the path to spiritual understanding. After the initial shock wears off—the shock that comes as a result of realizing that in order to walk the spiritual path in earnest you must be willing to take complete responsibility for your own life—there is often a period of significant advancement that ensues.

In my own life, my initial spiritual work resulted in a financially lucrative and professionally satisfying period that lasted for a number of years. When I finally realized that I was the one responsible for the quality of my own life, I worked hard to change myself into the person I wanted to be. For a solid year, I meditated every day, read books and attended workshops on spirituality, and when I became aware that my thoughts were gravitating toward the negative, I did my best to redirect them toward the positive. As a result, I found a great job with a tremendous amount of responsibility and was working for a wonderful boss who was encouraging and supportive. In addition, my confidence increased and my skills as a placement professional significantly improved, as did my bank account. Life was grand.

And then, as with Evan, my boss decided to leave the company.

THE STORM

Why, when things are going so well, when we're advancing by leaps and bounds, does life decide to pull the rug out from under us? To see what we're made of, to test our resolve— that's why. Since it's not a challenge to act like a Soul when things are going well, the only way to know how far you've come, as well as how far you have to go, is to see how you think and act when times get tough.

In metaphysical literature, this trying period in the life of a Soul is called "the storm, " or as St. John of the Cross called it, "the dark night of the soul." Most people don't see that the difficult problems and challenges that confront them in material reality, including on the job, are in truth spiritual crises. And, in my opinion, that's why most people don't ever find the peace, happiness, and success they deserve as spiritual beings.

Allow me to reiterate the basic premise of this book. There is only one life. Spirit or God is all that exists, therefore other people, places, situations, or things are illusions. External or material reality is the effect, and internal or spiritual reality is the cause. Nothing happens by accident. Nothing happens to you that you haven't attracted to yourself for a reason. The reason behind every occurrence—good, bad, or indifferent—is to evolve as a Soul.

The storm occurs when the mind, which is completely focused

on the past, clashes with the Soul, whose field of vision includes the past but whose focus is on the present and the future. In other words, when a change occurs in material reality for which an individual is unprepared, such as the sudden departure of a supervisor or boss, a war for control over the emotions breaks out between the mind and the Soul.

Back in Chapter 6, I related the story of how as I was trying to sublimate my anger into patience during a trying dinner conversation with friends, hives broke out all over the upper half of my body. These hives were the physical proof of the storm that was raging inside of me, of the war for control that was taking place between my mind and my Soul.

Evan's storm didn't have physical manifestations. His mind's reaction to his new supervisor's departure was projected back to him through his colleagues' negative reactions to the event. But even though his colleagues, and his mind, tried to get him to panic about the situation, his Soul prevailed, and Evan chose to have faith that the situation would resolve itself positively. It is sad that as long as the ramifications of an event are unclear, the majority of people will panic and anticipate the worst. The unknown is very frightening to those who are the prisoners of material reality. Therefore, the Soul who wishes to advance, in both the material as well as the spiritual worlds, must be ever watchful for any internal or external signs of inclement weather and take steps necessary to remain calm.

GOING IT ALONE

The moment Evan decided to have faith that everything would work out for the best, he separated himself from the rest of his colleagues. He was no longer one of the crowd. His decision to continue to think and act as a Soul meant that he would have to go it alone.

The greatest part of choosing to live as a Soul is that the rewards, both material and spiritual, are great. The hardest part, however, is that you have to do it by yourself. When the Buddha decided to renounce his worldly life as a prince and leave his father's kingdom to seek enlightenment, he had no choice but to leave his wife and his newborn son behind. The twelve apostles weren't crucified alongside Christ; he had to go alone. Likewise, we can't take anyone with us on our spiritual journey.

Everyone is evolving and growing at his or her own rate of speed. Who are we to assume that our path is the path for everyone? It is important to keep in mind that spirituality is incompatible with egotism. Just because we may have chosen to base our lives on spiritual principles doesn't mean that everyone else should do the same. We are not God's chosen people simply because we have decided to take some preliminary steps on the spiritual path. We should concern ourselves with practicing what we preach before trying to convince others of the validity of our approach to life.

This caveat against egotism notwithstanding, it takes great courage and endurance to go it alone. As anyone who has tried it knows, it isn't easy to have faith when the majority of people around you have succumbed to fear. Sometimes hope doesn't seem to be the appropriate response when events appear to be taking a turn for the worse. When those situations arise that tempt you to throw in your lot with the fearful and the worried, however, remember the divine law of cause and effect. If you want to harvest a crop of roses, don't plant weeds. If you want a positive outcome, leave your negative thoughts behind.

CREATING OPPORTUNITY

Because Evan endured as a Soul, he was able to turn an unclear situation into an opportunity. While everyone else was waiting to see what Eileen, the new supervisor, was going to do, Evan only concerned himself with what he was going to do. Because he was aligned with the power of the positive, he didn't see Eileen as a potential enemy, but rather as someone with whom he could develop a mutually satisfying working relationship. As a result, his positive attitude paid off. Eileen was more than happy to work with Evan because he was offering to fill a need in the department. She had nothing to lose by giving him a chance to prove that he was worthy of more responsibility.

As much as we overcomplicate matters in today's society, there really is no mystery to getting ahead on the job, and there never has been. Those people who get ahead know how to create opportunities for themselves by offering their services to life and to other people. It isn't necessary to be a genius to advance within the ranks. Contrary to conventional opinion, it is neither practical nor necessary to plot and scheme and step on and over coworkers and friends to move up the ladder. What you sow, so shall you reap. If you want to reap positive results in your life, go about doing positive things. Then you only need to have faith in yourself and the confidence to move ahead.

Over the years, I have worked with and supervised many people who desperately wanted to advance. But most of those people wanted to advance only to satisfy their egos. For a variety of reasons, they felt insecure and inferior and needed constant pats on the back from external reality to make them feel worthy. Unfortunately, however, no amount of recognition can turn a person who feels inferior into a self-assured, confident individual. The cause of insecurity comes from the inside, and so does the cure. The bottom line is that if you want to advance on the job or anywhere else, you first have to be willing to confront and change the beliefs that are holding you back, sometimes with expert help; second, you must step up to the plate and become an active participant in life.

Usually the people who advance on the job make it look effortless. They do their jobs well, look for opportunities to serve, and because they respect themselves as expressions of the One Life, of Spirit, they treat their supervisors, coworkers, and everyone else with respect. Because they know that they are responsible for the quality of their lives, they do not blame others when circumstances don't go their way. They call the shots; therefore, they can roll with the punches, knowing that they will advance when the time is right.

SELF-WORTH, ADVANCEMENT, AND MONEY

After Evan successfully proved to Eileen that he was the person to take charge of automating the departmental reports, he told her he was ready for even more responsibility and a higher salary. Now, here is where Evan could have lost his nerve by convincing himself that because he didn't have a college degree, he wasn't qualified to be promoted to a supervisory position or to receive a higher salary. But Evan didn't lose his nerve, and he didn't allow any old beliefs to dictate his actions. He knew that he could do the job, and because he had already proven his worth to Eileen, he was promoted and given a higher salary. His educational background was not even a factor in the decision to give him a significant raise.

Now, I'm not saying that some jobs don't require advanced training or education for good reasons. And I'm not saying that if you have a high school diploma and no additional training, you are qualified to practice medicine or law. What I am saying, however, is that you can only receive from life what you allow yourself to receive. If you see your qualifications in a negative light, so will everyone else, and the odds are great that you will not advance at the same rate as you will if you see yourself, your background, education, and life experience as unique, valuable, and useful. This same reasoning applies to money. If you believe that you are not worthy of a higher salary, you will not receive a higher salary. If you do not ask for more money, the odds are slim that your employer will decide out of the blue to give you a raise.

A few years ago right before Christmas, a married friend of mine with three small children was laid off from his well-paying job. Needless to say, his company's timing couldn't have been worse. But while quite a few people close to him panicked, my friend decided to enjoy the holidays and to begin his job search in the new year. Further, he decided to see the timing of the layoff as perfect because he had already decided that he was ready for a much better job and wanted to double his salary.

I must admit that when I found out about my friend's plan, I thought he had gone a little nuts. After all, hadn't he, like everyone else, been reading all those articles about the shrinking economy and the lack of opportunity? To make a long story short, much to my surprise, but not to his, after a four-month search my friend got the exact job he wanted and the precise amount of money he had requested. When I asked him how he did it, he said, "I was ready to move ahead. I'm great at what I do, so why shouldn't I have gotten what I wanted?"

ASSISTING OTHER SOULS ON THE PATH

There is another part to Evan's story that he neglected to include. After he was promoted to supervisor, Evan noticed that there was one administrative assistant on his staff who stood out among the rest. Hannah was a little shy, but her work was excellent. In addition, she always asked questions when she didn't understand how to complete a project, and she always met her deadlines. Evan knew that Hannah had what it took to succeed. But, like him when he first began working in the photocopy/duplication department, Evan knew that Hannah would need a mentor to show her the ropes. So, like his boss before him, Evan took Hannah under his wing.

Thanks to Evan, another Soul moved a little farther along on the path.

ELEVEN

FINDING THE WORK
YOU LOVE

As little children, most of us had the natural ability to dream about what we would do when we grew up. We played games where we acted out our most elaborate fantasies. We never felt compelled to stick with one fantasy for very long. One day we could be a policeman, the next a musician, and the next a mother or a father. Because we had so little life experience, time had no real meaning to us. Every day was a new day. Every day was a new opportunity to imagine a new life. We didn't feel the need to censor ourselves. We didn't have to ask ourselves if our dreams were practical or useful or whether or not we had enough talent to pursue them. We let ourselves go. We gave ourselves up to the present moment and to whatever idea popped into our heads. Because we were kids, we never felt the need to question our right to dream, to fantasize, or to play. Instinctively we knew that we were doing what we were supposed to do. For a while the adults left us alone, and sometimes they even joined in.

Then, something happened. We went to school. There was still enough time to play, create, and act out whatever came into our imaginations; but as life went on, there was less and less time for dreaming. There were decisions and choices to be made. We had to "buckle down." We had to get serious. We had to start thinking about tomorrow. We learned that we weren't going to live forever. We got the clear message that our lives weren't simply going to take care of themselves—we had to direct them. If we knew what was good for us, we would direct them to maximize our earning potential and minimize the time we spent enjoying ourselves. Before we knew it, all those activities that we loved as children either became hobbies that we had no time to pursue or became faint memories of a distant and carefree past.

Sound familiar? To a greater or lesser degree, each and every one of us has suffered from having to give up one or more of our dreams. Despite the fact that we say we don't care that we've had to do so in order to satisfy the authority figures in our lives, we really do care.

The crux of most career dilemmas boils down to the simple fact that many, if not most of us, are not doing work we want to do. Why not? Because we were discouraged from pursuing what we wanted because "it didn't pay," and as a result we became afraid to go against the tide, separate ourselves from the rest of the pack, and risk following our hearts.

Back in Chapter 3, I told the story of Meg, who had been unhappy in all of her jobs but couldn't understand why until she figured out that she had sacrificed her childhood dream of being an artist in order to make her parents happy. Even though Meg didn't realize it, she was a step ahead of a lot of people who are struggling to figure out what they want to do with their lives. At least she could remember what her childhood dream had been.

As a placement counselor, I worked with many people who insisted that they couldn't remember any childhood dreams whatsoever. It's as if their memories had been scraped clean of anything that came from their imaginations. Interestingly enough, these were the same people who insisted that they were not "creative" and that they didn't have any hobbies. But, even though I never let them know I didn't believe them, I knew that if they weren't creative on some level, if they didn't have any dreams or aspirations, they wouldn't care what kind of job they had. They certainly wouldn't have had the inclination to talk to me about their situation.

The point is, no matter how hard we try to fool ourselves into thinking that we have no dreams or aspirations, or how vehemently we insist that we are not creative, we are lying to ourselves. Even if our minds do not consciously know what we want to do with our lives, our Souls do. The more we allow ourselves to develop the spiritual aspect of our being, the safer it becomes to remember our dreams and to act on our creative inclinations— and the easier and more natural it becomes to succeed at a job we love.

Marilyn, age forty, had a successful career as a book editor and writer when she unexpectedly found herself without a job. While she was anxious about the situation, she decided to put her spiritual principles to work by allowing her Soul to lead her to her next job.

"When I first found out that I had lost my job, like most people I panicked. But luckily I had been laid off before, so I knew that it was possible to survive. This time I vowed to handle the situation more positively and to try not to fall victim to negative emotion. I also thought that I'd use this occasion to get a job that I would love, rather than one that would simply take care of my material needs.

"But the problem was that at this stage in my career, I didn't really know what kind of job would make me the happiest. So I decided to perform an experiment. The first thing I did was to ask my Soul to reveal any information that would help me to decide what my next career move should be. I decided to not limit myself to any particular field. I would consider any career path my Soul could come up with. And even though it was incredibly difficult to restrain my anxiety, I gave myself two full weeks for this part of the process.

"Whenever an idea came to me that struck me as career-related, I wrote it down, even if it seemed strange or impractical. In addition, every morning I tried to remember any dreams I had the night before, and when I could remember one, I wrote it down. A little later, I read what I had written and sometimes I was surprised to find the dream seemed to contain a message for me from my unconscious mind. During the two weeks when I wasn't recording ideas and dream messages, I let myself enjoy myself. At first it was difficult. But after three or four days, my body began to slow down, and my mind began to cooperate with me because it didn't have anything else to do. Around the twelfth day of my experiment, I realized that I was in the right field, but in the wrong job. I enjoyed being a book editor, but I didn't like the company where I was working or the kinds of books I had been editing. In addition, I felt that I was ready to move up the ladder into a job with more responsibility. It became clear to me that I wanted to get a job as an editor that would lead to an editor-in-chief position, I wanted to edit spiritually oriented books, and I wanted the same or better money than I had been making at my last job before the layoff.

"I formed a mental image of the job I wanted and recreated this image at least twice a day. I also wrote a short affirmation to remind me of my image and I repeated it to myself as often as I needed to keep me on the right track. A week later, I decided, even though money was tight, to attend the annual convention of booksellers. I took a ton of résumés with me and almost as soon as I entered the convention I felt 'called' to a specific booth. I introduced myself to the woman at the booth and calmly explained that I was 'drawn' to her company. The woman smiled, told me that her name was Linda and that she was the owner of the publishing company, which was located in the Midwest. To my surprise, I realized that she was the author of one of my favorite books on spirituality. We talked for a while, I gave her my résumé, and she said that she'd be in touch.

"One day several months later, I received a call from Linda's company inviting me to take on a few projects on a freelance basis. Shortly after I finished the projects, I was hired as editor-in-chief and moved to the 'heartland of America.' Even though I had a job offer in New York City for twice the money, I knew that I had found my calling. I also knew that working with Linda was an opportunity I couldn't pass up. By keeping the faith and letting my Soul lead the way, I found my dream job and the people who would support me on the next leg of my spiritual journey."

CREATIVE PARTICIPATION

Many of us say we want a better job, but few of us are willing to do what needs to be done to get one. In fact, many of us would scoff at the process Marilyn used to find work she loved. Regardless of the excuses and opinions we can come up with to rationalize our laziness and complacency, however, there is no getting around the fact that life is a participatory process, and participation is creation. Sitting on the couch and watching hour after hour of television or spending all our free time on the phone reliving the day's irritations with our friends is not going to bring us a better life.

If we want to get a job that we love, the first thing we need to do is to stop feeling sorry for ourselves and blaming other people for the situation we are in and take matters into our own hands. No one is going to come galloping into our living room on a white horse with the answers to life's mysteries or to our career dilemmas. Like Marilyn, we must get out of panic mode and into action mode. Keep in mind, however, that if you are suffering from severe or chronic depression, taking action might require seeking expert professional help. Most of us get trapped in the maze of our minds from time to time. Seeking help to resolve emotional or psychological problems is an act of great strength and is not anti-spiritual. Rather, for many it is a necessary part of the spiritual process.

Once in action mode, we need to decide to replace any thoughts we may have that are inspired by fear, anger, and worry with thoughts inspired by faith, patience, and hope. Like attracts like. A wonderful job opportunity is not going to materialize for someone who is miserable and unhappy. It can't and won't happen. Therefore, when misery and unhappiness threaten to overtake us, we need to stop and remind ourselves that we are not victims of life; we are spiritual beings. We are co-creators with life, Spirit, or God. Each and every one of us *can* work at a job we love. First we have to have the courage to find out what kind of job we want. In order to do this, we must figure out a way to bypass the mind with its negative attitude and connect with our Souls, the guardians of our imaginations.

ASKING FOR GUIDANCE

I know that I could have avoided much hardship in my life if I had allowed myself to ask for guidance from my Soul. But as a highly trained mind, I believed that going within for guidance was showing weakness. In trying to prove that I was tough and could take anything that life could offer, I was really proving that I had no clue who I really was; that is, a spiritual being and not a collection of thoughts and opinions housed in a physical form. It does not show strength to believe that you and your little ego can handle anything that comes your way. It is foolish.

The universe operates according to rational and logical principles and laws, but the fulfillment of these laws is impersonal. For example, as my friend and teacher Jackie Kayata always says, if a really good person and a really bad person decide to jump off a cliff, the universe isn't going to save the good person and kill the bad person. The law of gravity doesn't care about whether you're good or bad, it just works. The same holds true for the law of cause and effect. If you go about acting stubborn and pigheaded, assuming that you have all the answers to life, your Soul has no cause to reveal itself to you even if you have the highest IQ on the planet. If you adopt an open attitude, however, and if you believe that you may have a thing or two to learn about yourself and the nature of reality, then your Soul can't help but begin to move from out of the shadows of your being into the light of your awareness.

It doesn't matter in the least what term you use to describe the act of asking for guidance from your Soul. Some people call it prayer. Others call it meditation or receptive visualization. What does matter is that it works. If you can suspend your disbelief, even temporarily, and put your faith in the one life of Spirit, you *will* find the answers that you seek.

Now, let's review the procedure that Marilyn followed to figure out her next career move. First of all, she asked her Soul to reveal any information to her that would help her to find a job that she would love. Then, after opening a channel to her higher self, she allotted two weeks to see what information was revealed to her either in the waking or dream state. Most importantly, Marilyn realized that if she really wanted positive and helpful information from her Soul, she couldn't walk around in a funk.

Even though it wasn't easy, she sent her mind on vacation and decided to enjoy herself for the duration of her experiment.

It is important to keep in mind that when you first start going inward for guidance, information from your Soul may not be communicated to you in the most direct and readily comprehensible manner. As I've said before, taking the first steps on the spiritual path is very similar to learning to speak and understand a foreign language. Until you get used to the accent of native speakers and develop a big enough vocabulary to have a conversation, you have to rely on facial expressions and physical gestures to communicate. And, as anyone who has ever traveled knows, the more relaxed you are when trying to communicate in a foreign language, the more successful you usually are.

The key to "getting the message," is to become like a child. Have fun and let your imagination help you out. If you have an interesting dream, or an idea pops into your head, write it down. If you feel like drawing a picture, draw whatever comes into your head. If you have the urge to read a particular book, call someone on the phone, listen to music you haven't listened to in years, do it. Don't judge your inclinations, act on them. When doubts surface that you can't communicate with the Spirit within through your Soul, gently remind yourself of your divine birthright, "Seek and you shall find. Knock and it shall be opened unto you. Ask and you shall receive."

THE IDEA

After receiving the information from her Soul that she requested, Marilyn realized that while she wasn't in the wrong career, she was definitely in the wrong job. Intuitively she knew that what she really wanted was a job with more responsibility that would lead to an editor-in-chief position that would allow her to edit books on spirituality. Now that she had formulated a new idea, she had a new direction and a new vision for her life.

All creation begins with an idea. If you want to change your career direction, you have to be willing to create a new idea based on the information you've received, consciously or unconsciously, from your real self, your Soul. This new idea will become your guiding vision, your blueprint, your plan. Ideas are powerful. If we nurture negative ideas with our thoughts for a long enough period of time, we create hellish conditions in our lives. If we nurture positive ideas, we create heavenly circumstances.

If you want to know what your guiding vision has been up to now, take a look at your life. All the aspects of your life—what you have and don't have—have come to you, or not, lawfully, via the law of cause and effect, from your guiding vision. This vision is the result of your desires and your beliefs. It is impossible to fulfill a desire if you do not believe that you have a right to fulfill it, if you are unwilling to take the necessary steps to achieve it, or if you are unable to accept it once it has manifested in material reality. Regardless of what conventional wisdom or religious dogma may lead you to believe, there is only one thing standing between you and what you want, and that is fear. As we now know, however, there is a tried and true antidote to fear, and it is faith.

DESIRE, FEELING, AND FAITH

When I first became a placement counselor, I had no idea just how spiritual the whole process of finding someone a job was. But after I got the hang of it, I began to see that if I really liked a candidate who needed or wanted a new job, I would find that person a job. Likewise, if I was intrigued or fascinated by a job that a client needed to fill, I would find the perfect candidate for the job. Eventually I realized that I had discovered the secret to success, the recipe for actualizing a personal vision: strong desire, feeling, and faith. Whenever these three ingredients were present, Spirit always brought me either the right job or the right candidate at exactly the right time.

One day I met with a candidate, Jim, whom I really liked. He was smart, personable, and had a great background. In addition, he struck me as the type of person who helped other people out whenever he could. He told me that he was happy where he was working, but that he'd be interested if an "unusual" job came across my desk. Something told me that I would find him the perfect job.

A few weeks later, I got a call from a law firm, who wasn't a regular client, asking if I had any candidates who might be interested in working in their London office. The client explained that they usually filled these kinds of positions from within, but for some reason there were no suitable in-house candidates this time around. The type of person and the kind of background they were looking for fit Jim to a tee. I could barely contain my excitement as I hung up on the client and called Jim. He was thrilled. He told me that he had always wanted to work abroad.

The client met with several candidates, but there was really never any doubt that Jim would get the job. It was meant for him, and even though he didn't know it, he helped to create it. While Jim wasn't consciously aware that he had been nurturing the idea of living abroad, his desire was obviously very strong, so strong that when the conditions were right, the Spirit within granted his wish.

FORMING AN IMAGE

If you really think about it, you'll probably be forced to admit that you have received many of the things you've asked for in life. But you probably don't know how these things actually got to you. The creation process is so automatic that we don't really stop to understand how ideas, wants, and desires materialize in our lives.

Jim's story is a perfect example of how the process works. First we get an idea, such as that we'd like to work abroad. Then, because we have complete faith that it would be possible to work abroad, because lots of people do, and because we have such a strong desire for our idea to come to life, we imagine what it would be like if it did happen. Eventually our conscious minds forget about the idea, and we go about living our lives. But from time to time we daydream about living and working in a foreign country and sometimes we even dream about it while we are asleep. Then minutes, days, months, years, or even decades after we had the idea, Spirit, who has been working on the idea all along, determines that the conditions for the manifestation of our dream are right, and we find that our idea has become a reality.

This is how ideas come alive. As I said before, this process is automatic and mostly unconscious. But if you want to take direct and conscious control over the creation process, if you'd like to start right now to find work you love, you need only continue to follow Marilyn's procedure. The next step is learning how to form an image of what you desire and allowing yourself to bask in the feeling that comes when you know that you are going to get exactly what you want.

An image is nothing more than a mental picture of your idea that you create using your imagination. When you form an image and regularly focus your attention on it, it's as if you are sending a video or a detailed photograph of what you want to Spirit to ensure that you get it exactly as desired. Images can be elaborate or simple, but the more details you are able to provide, the closer your reality will match your image. Here is the procedure I follow when forming an image:

Step 1: Write It Down

It is much easier to form a mental picture of something if you write it down first. The act of writing it down forces you to focus all your attention on your desire and gives you the opportunity to edit it until it is exactly the way you want it to be. If you want a positive opportunity, such as a job that you love, to manifest in your life, your image has to be written using positive energy. You are imaging or visualizing a perfect opportunity. Your doubts, fears, and negative thoughts have no place in your image.

In addition, remember that Spirit is not concerned with the past or the future. It lives and works in the eternal present. Therefore, your image should be stated in the present tense, as if what you want to occur is happening right now. One more thing, your image has to be logical. If you are currently an entry-level administrative assistant, it isn't realistic to form an image that within three weeks you will be President of the United States. It is possible, however, to create an image that within a reasonable amount of time you will work in the industry of your choice, for a fabulous boss, performing work that is stimulating and receiving a great salary that adequately takes care of all your material needs.

To give you an idea of how to write an image, here is a short one that I created when I got the idea to write this book, which I knew would be work that I would love.

I am so excited that I am writing *Your Life's Work*, a book on how to use spiritual principles to create a satisfying and successful work life. Thanks to the efforts of my literary agent, a wonderful and supportive person, *Your Life's Work* is being published by a major publishing company. I am very happy with my new career as a full-time writer. Paid writing and editing assignments come to me easily, and I am earning enough money to take care of all my material needs with plenty to spare. I get out of bed every morning thrilled to sit down at my new computer and begin writing. All of my friends and family are very supportive of my new career and are very generous with their love and encouragement. Thank you, life, for providing me with such a wonderful and challenging opportunity!

Step 2: See Your Image in Your Mind

When I first form an image, I record myself reading my written image out loud on tape. Then I get in a comfortable position, relax my body completely, close my eyes, and listen to my tape over and over until I can see my image in my mind. After I've formed a mental picture of my image, I focus on it for as long as I can. While I'm focusing on the image, I gradually try to add other sensory impressions, such as what I would hear, smell, taste, and touch if my image were real, and even more importantly, I use my imagination to begin to feel the emotions associated with my image. For example, if I were to be offered a job I would love, I would be happy, peaceful, joyful, and lighthearted. I remain in this quiet, yet emotionally charged state for as long as I can.

Some people might have an easier time hearing an image than seeing one. This is fine. You don't have to literally "see" an image to visualize it. All you need to do is to imagine that whatever you want to occur is happening in the present moment. Don't be critical of your ability to visualize a scenario. As time goes on, your ability to use all your senses in the imaging process will improve. The most important parts of imaging or visualizing are to decide what it is that you want, to have faith that you will get it, and to allow yourself to feel as if what you want is happening in the present moment.

FOCUS

Repetition is the key to effective imaging. When I want something to manifest in my life, I make sure to take time at least twice a day, once in the morning right after I wake up and once right before I fall asleep, to recreate and visualize my image. Then, as I proceed with my day, I try to monitor myself every so often to make sure that I'm not thinking thoughts, talking, or acting in a manner that is contrary to the way I would think, talk, and act if I my desire had been fulfilled. If I want a job that I would love to manifest in my life, for example, I can't go around thinking, talking, or acting as if I hate my current job. My intention is to love working; therefore, complaining about how much I hate my job is sending the wrong message to Spirit.

Of course it is not possible to totally eradicate every negative thought during the day. Therefore, it is helpful to write a one- or two-line affirmation that you can repeat to yourself when you feel yourself slipping away from your goal. I used to repeat, "I love my job. I'm happy, relaxed, and at peace," over and over to myself when things started slipping out of control. It's a simple technique, but it works to bring you back to where you want to be.

If you really want to impress Spirit with your intention to get a job that you'll love, take some action in that direction. After Marilyn formed her image of the job she wanted, she didn't go on vacation. After all, she didn't just want a job that she loved, she needed one immediately in order to meet her financial commitments. So, full of faith and armed with her résumé, she went to the annual convention of booksellers and let her Soul direct her where she needed to go. Because she had established her intention to find a job as an editor of spiritually oriented books, thanks to the law of cause and effect, she was led to the booth of a company that published spiritual books. But she wasn't offered a job on the spot. She had to continue to act in order to get the job. Because she was determined to fulfill her desire, however, her actions paid off. Creation is a participatory process. If you want something, you've got to believe that you deserve it, and most importantly, you must be willing to go and get it.

MANIFESTATION

Often the hardest part of the creation process is the actual manifestation of your dream. Because of fear, it isn't always easy to accept opportunities when they come to you. That is why faith is so integral to the imaging process. The most important kind of faith to develop is faith in yourself, your real self, your Soul. It's not enough to create an image of a better life. You have to have faith that you can live a better life, and be willing to accept the gifts life offers you.

Faith is also important because sometimes what you *think* you want is not what your Soul *knows* you want. Often what manifests from your image is even better than what you expected, but without faith that your Soul and Spirit know what they are doing, you might miss a great opportunity just because it isn't exactly what you had in mind.

When my sister was a junior in high school, she wanted to spend the summer in a foreign country as an exchange student. She applied to the organization that was sponsoring the exchange program and was confident that she would be accepted because of her background, her grades, her recommendations, and her ability to get along well with people. In fact, our entire family thought that she was a shoo-in and waited eagerly for the letter of acceptance to arrive in the mail. When the letter arrived, my sister discovered, much to her surprise, that she had not been accepted into the program. For a few weeks, our entire family was depressed.

Then, a month or two later, one of my sister's teachers gave her an application for a summer scholarship to the Pennsylvania Governor's School for the Arts. He told her that no one from our high school had ever been selected, but he thought she should audition to see what would happen. My sister, who was and is very talented in many of the arts and was considering pursuing an artistic career, decided to audition as an actress and prepared a monologue. Several weeks later, she was elated to find out that she had been selected to receive a scholarship.

Sometimes what looks like a major disappointment is really a blessing in disguise. If your image does not materialize exactly the way you want, either the time is not yet right for it to manifest, or something better is on the way.

LIFE IS A WORK IN PROGRESS

Your life is your artistic masterpiece, but no great masterpiece was completed in a day. Marilyn discovered that she had the wrong job but was in the right industry, so her image manifested very quickly. What if you are currently a secretary and discover that you want to be an obstetrician? The creation process is always the same no matter what you want to create. The amount of time an image takes to manifest in material reality, however, varies from image to image; and no image is going to manifest without your participation. Take some action in the direction you want to go in, and the powerful but invisible force of Spirit will guide you where you need to go.

You can get what you want out of life, but sometimes delays and detours along the way are necessary to make the journey more enjoyable or meaningful. Every moment is full of unlimited opportunity for joy. Relax, you'll find what you are looking for. In the meantime, if you're not yet in a job you love, love the job you're in.

of being. When we set our sights on a new job, more money, a new car, a bigger house, or a better or more fulfilling relationship, what we are really asking for is happiness, which is a very worthy goal. In fact, it is the only goal really worth pursuing.

Some religious dogma might expound on the beauty and necessity of suffering and misery, but even a glimmer of spiritual truth reveals that joy not pain, love not hate, happiness not misery is our true emotional state as living Souls. This state, where joy, love, and happiness transcend all other emotions, brings with it direct knowledge of Spirit or God and is called cosmic consciousness or the kingdom of heaven. Despite what we may have heard to the contrary, it is not necessary to physically die to experience this spiritual state. We can experience it right here and now. In fact, to aspire to cosmic consciousness is to aspire to success. To achieve cosmic consciousness is to achieve success.

To be truly successful is to know that Spirit or God created life, sustains life, and is life itself. It was never born and can never die. It is self-nurturing and self-fulfilling. It has no desires because it has no needs. It is everything and nothing at the same time. It is the ultimate good because it exists only to give, and it gives to all living things, equally and without judgment. To be successful is to understand that we are Souls, living expressions of this essence, agents of the ultimate good. To be successful is to possess the quiet confidence and the great strength of character that comes with the knowledge that we have the power to satisfy all our needs and desires because we are the sons and daughters of Spirit, of God, and are nourished and affirmed by life itself.

Our material reality results from our spiritual reality. Therefore, pursuing spiritual knowledge and understanding is the most practical and direct path to take if success on any level—material, emotional, or spiritual—is the goal. It makes no difference whether our desire is to own a luxury car or to attain inner peace. Spirit does not judge our needs or desires, it simply gives us what we ask for through the mechanism of our thoughts, our words, and our actions.

If we truly desire success, we can have it. But we must be willing and able to define it for ourselves, do what is necessary in order to get it, and, most importantly, be able to accept it and help others to achieve it.

David, age thirty-three, is a vice president in an investment firm and earns a six-figure income. As his family was not affluent, he attended college on a football scholarship and worked in a variety of different jobs during the school year and summers while maintaining excellent grades. Ever since junior high school, Dave had been interested in finance and had dreamed of becoming an investment executive. After college he decided to pursue his dream. On the recommendation of some college alumni, he interviewed at several brokerage and investment firms and after a few months landed a job as a trader. Five years later, he was recruited and hired by a major investment firm that paid for him to get his MBA. After finishing graduate school, David was promoted and is now responsible for managing a department within his firm.

"When I first got out of college, my goal was to become successful by earning a lot of money. But I grew up in a family where money was not thought of in a positive manner and where people who made a lot of money were not considered favorably. As a result of my negative ideas about wealth, I continually questioned my worthiness to have material success even after I landed my first job as a trader and was on the road to achieving my goal.

"I found myself in a strange predicament. Even though I loved my work and was good at making money for myself and for other people, as my bank account increased, so did my nagging fear that I was somehow doing something wrong. That feeling kept me from being happy. One day when I was good and tired of feeling depressed about being financially successful, a friend of mine suggested that what I was undergoing was in actuality a spiritual crisis. She suggested that I reevaluate my philosophy of life and learn to accept and share my wealth, rather than judge and malign it. What she said seemed a little too 'new agey' for a serious person like myself, but, as I said, I was tired of being unhappy for being good at making money and decided to take her advice.

"After I became involved in spirituality, I realized that even though I had been confusing money with happiness, making money and pursuing wealth are not inherently bad. Money is simply one manifestation of the abundance of the universe. And despite what most people think, there is plenty to go around. I also decided that since I already knew how to take care of my financial needs, I should now concentrate on achieving happiness, which for me is true success.

"Recently, my life changed dramatically when my wife and I had a baby. I feel fortunate that I don't have to pass on my old negative beliefs about money to my child. I'd like this little creature of the universe to grow up knowing that life is about abundance, not lack. I'd like her to know from the start what it took me many years to find out, that the Soul's journey is about pursuing what makes you happy and using wealth, material or spiritual, to help anyone and everyone to fulfill their dreams and their potential as spiritual beings."

SCARCITY VS. ABUNDANCE

I have known Dave a long time and what I admire most about him is his generosity and his open-mindedness regarding using spiritual principles to overcome his negative feelings about money and wealth. Many, if not most, people have a problem with money and achieving affluence but balk at the notion that a spiritual approach might provide the solution to their problems. What these people do not understand is that their beliefs about the nature of reality are what is holding them back from getting what they say they want. Even though there are plenty of indications that the tide is turning in a spiritual direction, the majority of people still see spirituality as mumbo jumbo spouted by weak people who don't have enough common sense or brain power to figure out how the world really works—that is, in a dog-eat-dog fashion.

Sadly enough, those same people, even the ones who consider themselves to be devoutly religious, spend much of their time and energy either hating the rich or despising the poor. Why? Because it is easier to hate or fear other people than it is to take responsibility for one's own life. So, whether these people have money or they don't, their lives are based on the philosophy of lack, meaning that regardless of how much money they have in the bank, they never feel satisfied. Their lives are based on the cruel and unrelenting belief that they are not worthy of having enough. When you believe that you will never have enough, you feel as if you have no other choice but to claw and scratch your way along life's path, exploiting everything and everyone around you in a futile attempt to fulfill your needs.

We all suffer to some degree from this terrible malaise, because unknowingly we have all been indoctrinated to believe in the economic principle of scarcity, the by-product of the mechanistic worldview ushered in by the scientific revolution. The message inherent in this ugly doctrine is that there are not adequate resources available to sustain everyone on the planet, hence we must all compete fiercely to get our share at the expense of everyone else.

This principle is based on the notion that greed is the underlying emotion motivating all members of our species. As a consequence of this rampant and supposedly "natural" greed, it is inevitable from an economic standpoint that a portion of the human population will suffer from poverty and lack, living out their destinies as casualties in the economic struggle of the survival of the fittest.

Despite the bleak landscape of this spiritless and ill-conceived Darwinian nightmare, we are led to believe that the concept of scarcity is a good thing because it encourages individuals to compete for the best life has to offer. In and of itself, competition is not a negative concept. After all, competition often results in increased knowledge, better wages, and new and improved methods of production. Unfortunately, however, a wholesale belief in scarcity and in unbridled competition wreaks havoc on the planet.

In a culture where belief in scarcity dictates that there is not enough for everyone, fear drives the economic system. The by-products of fear are hate, war, instability, and ultimately insanity. The haves are separated from the have-nots. The strong claim the lion's share of the planet's resources for themselves and dole out whatever is left over to the weak. Value is based on the amount of material wealth accumulated. Nothing else is factored into the equation. In this godless and loveless universe, "he who dies with the most toys wins."

The desperate attempt to acquire more of everything is simply the external expression of every human being's internal yearning to reunite with Spirit, which is everything, and to find unconditional and infinite love and acceptance on the most profound and meaningful of levels. Without love and acceptance, the material world is a prison. In our evolutionary quest to make life easier through our obsessive enslavement to technology, we have not made it any happier. The horrible price that humanity has paid for deifying the material world is the loss of its connection to the divine, to God, to its own true nature.

There is another lens through which to view life and the universe, however, and that is the eyes of the Soul. These eyes are not restricted to seeing what seems to be real, what has already come into form. These eyes see beyond the form to the very essence that created the form. Since this essence, Spirit, God, or energy is all present, powerful, and knowing, these eyes can see that scarcity or lack is but an illusion, an obstacle that must be surmounted in order for our species to make the next evolutionary leap.

Abundance, not scarcity or lack, is our real birthright. Greed creates shortages, scarcity, and lack and is the result of our fear that we will not get our fair share. But in our hearts we all know that greed is an impractical and destructive response to life and that fear can only beget fear. Faith and kindness create miracles by stimulating the imagination and creative thought of the human Soul. When the Soul is creatively stimulated, answers to even the most difficult of problems surface, even those nagging and mysterious economic problems that plague mankind.

We often forget that the study of economics is a social science, like anthropology, sociology, and psychology, and as such seeks to understand the forces that influence and result from a culture's belief structure. A culture does not exist independently of its belief structure. We are, as a people and as individuals, the sum total of our beliefs. On an economic level, practicing abundant thinking would focus on serving life rather than fearing and thus destroying it, and would enhance competition with cooperation. As a consequence, a new reality would be revealed from which a true marketplace would evolve which could not sacrifice the death of even one child to the god of scarcity and fear in the name of economic progress.

Global economic mind change notwithstanding, on a personal level, abundant thinking is the answer to achieving success on any level. As a result of the law of cause and effect, what we believe to be true comes true. What we believe is possible becomes possible. If we want success, we have to believe that we are worthy of success, and that means replacing a belief in failure and lack with a belief in abundance and success. That means confronting our relationship with that old devil money.

THE EVOLVING SOUL AND MONEY

For most people, success and money go hand in hand. This is completely understandable given that as humans we do have certain material needs that need to be satisfied, and in most cases meeting these needs requires money. Unfortunately, however, money and affluence elude many of us because we are tremendously ambivalent about the subject. But if we want to achieve the success we say we want, we need to forget, if only temporarily, any preconceived notions we have about money and try to look at the subject with a little objectivity.

I remember the first time my metaphysics teacher, Dr. Kayata, asked me, "If you didn't have a body, would you have any material needs? Would you need money?" I thought about it and realized that the answer was no, if I didn't have a body, I wouldn't need anything. I would be a completely spiritual being with no material needs or desires whatsoever. Then it dawned on me. I *am* a spiritual being. In the most profound sense, I *am* a Soul, *not* a body. So if I believe that in the big scheme of things I'm not what I appear to be in material reality, then neither is money.

Let's begin our discussion by trying to figure out what money is. First of all, unlike water, air, or sunlight, money is an invention of the human mind. It is a concept that sprang from a brilliant and practical idea about how to make fulfilling the material needs of life easier. When you stop to think about it, the way that we think about and use money is a very recent phenomenon and is the outgrowth of the tremendous economic development of the last hundred years.

The moment the first human became self-aware, he or she didn't immediately rush out to the bank to open a checking account. It goes without saying that at the beginning of human life on the planet, MasterCard and VISA didn't exist. Self-sufficiency was the name of the game, and every individual or family was responsible for meeting its own material needs, including food, clothing, and shelter.

Eventually, however, for survival reasons, families began to band together to form communities to pool their resources. As these communities grew and human knowledge expanded, people began to specialize in particular jobs, such as farming or raising animals, and the barter system came into being as a method to exchange goods and services within the community. But as humans began to travel beyond the boundaries of their communities, they came in contact with other cultures and were exposed to new and different goods and services. With the development of trade between distant communities and cultures it became obvious that the barter system was a cumbersome, imprecise, and inconvenient way to transact business. Out of the need for an improved method of exchange came the invention of money. Money, therefore, facilitated trade, which facilitated exposure to still more humans and more cultures. While this exposure sometimes brought out the differences between people and cultures, which led to war and strife, at the same time it also led to a greater understanding of life as a result of the artistic and philosophical exchange that naturally occurred.

The invention of money was a necessary evolutionary step. Because of money, humans began to begin to think abstractly and conceptually, which stimulated the growth of imagination. We take money so much for granted that we can't conceive of a life without it. But imagine a farmer's shock the first time that someone handed him a few coins rather than two pigs for a bushel of wheat. In one instant the farmer's life was changed forever, because he was forced to understand that the coins symbolized two pigs, were the abstract equivalent of two pigs, which he could now use to buy a cow or something else he needed to survive.

In addition, before the invention of money, the job you did was usually determined by tradition. If your father was a farmer, most likely you became a farmer, too. Your imagination could not conceive of doing anything else, nor was there any need to do anything else. With the development of a monetary system came a more complex marketplace and new and different jobs, occupations, and professions. Even though you might have to struggle against family or community opposition, your occupation was now a matter of choice. With the growth of the economic marketplace, thanks to money, you could now pick a job that was more lucrative or more in keeping with your talents.

Money, therefore, served to help humans become more mobile, which stimulated creativity and inquisitiveness, which led to increased occupational choices and the desire to understand one's place in the cosmos, which has led us to our current study of spirituality. The bottom line, then, is that without money, I wouldn't be writing this book, and you wouldn't be reading it. In other words, it's not money but our attitude about making money that creates a problem.

Like Dave, I grew up in a family that did not have a high opinion of money or people who had money. But, unlike Dave, I didn't have any desire to pursue affluence or to develop the ability to make money until after I had begun working in the real world for several years. Until that time, like many people, I had a false sense of superiority because the focus of my life was not on making money. I now see that not making money didn't make me a better person, it just made me a person who never had much more money than she needed to pay her bills and take the occasional vacation.

No matter what we have been trained to believe, lack of money and spirituality do not go hand in hand. Money is not a moral issue. How a person uses or abuses money may have moral implications, but money in and of itself has as much or as little meaning as any other concept or idea that humans have come up with so far. The bottom line is that making money is a skill like any other, nothing more and nothing less. Dave wasn't born knowing how to make money. He had to learn how to do it. If we want to learn to make money, we have to do likewise.

As I have previously indicated in an earlier chapter, when I first became an executive recruiter or a "headhunter," I stunk at the job because something deep within me resisted not only learning how to sell, but also focusing on abundance and taking responsibility for my own financial status. After several painful months of not making much money, I realized, much to my chagrin, that I was a lot more comfortable allowing my employer to determine my financial worth than I was setting my own financial goals and taking the steps necessary to meet them. When you work on commission, as I did, that's not the best attitude to have.

I can now see that something inside me was urging me to let go of my old, outmoded beliefs about money, because eventually I was faced with the choice of allowing myself to sink into financial ruin or learning how to make money. Luckily, and it was touch and go for a while, I finally decided on the latter course of action. It was slow going at first, but eventually I began making very good money. How did I do it? The answer is simple. I let go of fear, acted as if I were the successful, confident, competent person I wanted to be, and began focusing my attention on making, not judging, money. I also did exactly what my boss told me to do. After all, she was financially successful, and I wasn't.

The keys to making money are to believe that you are worthy of it—which everyone is—to learn from someone who knows how to make it, and to have complete faith that you will get it. At the beginning of the process you may not have any idea how you'll find the right teacher or how the money is going to come to you. That's fine. Focus your attention on the object of your desire, become one with it, and opportunities to make money will come your way, sometimes in strange ways, via the law of cause and effect.

It seems to be a cosmic law (really just lack of patience, I guess) that everything in life takes longer than we humans think it should. Unfortunately, sometimes the money threatens to run out right before the thing you want is ready to manifest. I was faced with this scenario not long ago while writing this book. Even though I thought that I had budgeted enough money to devote all of my time to writing for a given length of time, some unexpected delays and expenses cropped up that threatened my plan and my financial stability. To make matters worse, I figured out just how bad things were right as I was about to go on vacation. I was worried, but decided to go on vacation anyway with the hope that something would happen to make things a little easier when I got back. I had no idea what this "something" would be since nobody owed me any money, but I kept telling myself that I should start having a little of the faith that I enjoyed telling everyone else so much about.

During my vacation and for several weeks afterward, I struggled to replace worry with hope and fear with faith. Some days were easier than others, but I persevered. Every time a negative thought entered my head, I mentally said something positive to myself. I continually counted my blessings. I made lists of all the things for which I had to be thankful. Then one day the phone rang, and the voice on the other end of the line told me that I was the first-place winner in a sweepstakes that I had entered the year before. I almost fainted when the voice told me that I had just won $5,000.

The funny thing was that even though I've entered a zillion sweepstakes in my life, I specifically remembered entering this particular sweepstakes because I thought the cash prize amounts—$25,000 grand prize, $5,000 first prize, $1,000 second prize, and $300 third prize—were "winnable." I remember filling out the entry form and thinking, *I could definitely win one of these prizes.* My belief must have been pretty strong because I did win. And was I happy that I did, because that money couldn't have come at a better time.

Learning how to make or attract money is important because with this knowledge comes the confidence that you can always meet your material needs. Let's face it, it's not easy to make the decision to pursue a lifelong dream when you are worried about paying the rent or buying groceries. But if you know that you are worthy of having money and believe that somehow your needs will be taken care of, it is easier to do what you really want to do with your life.

Your material circumstances, and your reaction to them, are a reflection of your level of spiritual understanding. When you feel that you have to focus all your time and energy on satisfying your material needs, your inner self, your nature as a Soul, languishes. When you are out of touch with your spiritual nature, happiness, which is true success, eludes you. When you aren't happy, you are unable to live your life the way you want. Many of us rationalize not doing what we want to do because we've been programmed to believe that we won't be able to make ends meet if we do. Once we learn how to make and attract money, we can't use that old tired excuse anymore. We might just have to get out there and do what it is we're on this planet to do.

LIVING FROM THE HEART

There are no accidents. Each and every one of us is on this planet for a reason. Our goal as individuals is to find out what that reason is and to do our utmost to use our talents to serve life. Since you are reading this book, and presumably other books with a spiritual theme, the odds are that your spiritual development is of greater importance to you than theirs may be to the majority of your friends and family. Like Dave, for you success on one level might mean financial affluence, but on another it means the freedom to live your life the way you want and to achieve happiness. Fortunately the way to achieve both of these kinds of success is to live from the heart, which means living from the Soul.

Everyone is walking the spiritual path, whether we are conscious of it as individuals or not. When we become conscious that we are on the path, when we become aware of something burning deep within us that cannot be satisfied in any material way whatsoever, a longing for total and complete union and peace, our spiritual development quickens, and we realize what we've known all along: We are the masters of our own destinies. We are in charge of our reality.

Free will means the ability to choose. We can see material suffering, deprivation, and lack all around us or we can see with the eyes of the Soul and focus our attention on the abundance and the love of Spirit or God that envelops and nurtures us and gives us whatever we want. We can live in heaven or we can live in hell. We can create miracles for ourselves and those around us and solve problems that seem unsolvable, or we can destroy ourselves and the beautiful and bountiful planet we live on. The decision whether to serve life or to destroy life is up to each of us to make.

To serve is to lead, but before we can serve others we must serve our higher natures, and that means doing what we want to do with our lives. Forget the rules. Let your imagination lead you where it wants to go and you will unblock creative energy to the intensity of which you have never seen before. Dream big and then make a logical plan to make your dream come true. Get going even if that means taking one very minor step in that direction. Have sympathy and compassion for those people who tell you that what you want to do can't be done. Instead of arguing with them, smile and ask them what they have always wanted to do. Then encourage them to do it and turn your attention back to manifesting your dream.

Your dreams will change as you change. Don't panic. Your Soul may have other even greater plans for you that you can't possibly imagine at the outset of your conscious journey of discovery. Seek happiness by being happy. When you get discouraged, take a break from yourself and volunteer to help someone achieve something they've always wanted to achieve. Giving and receiving are the two sides of abundance. When financial affluence comes your way, accept it and then share it. Spread it around. Use it to create joy and have no fear. Daily living has its ups and downs, but when you are committed to living as a Soul, life really does take care of itself.

My very dear friend Maya and I met when we were studying with the same voice teacher. We liked each other immediately and because we had so much in common, we quickly became friends. Maya had worked in many different jobs and had explored a variety of career directions, but her passions were singing, music, and spirituality. Maya is a very creative and talented person but also has a keen intellect. Her dilemma had always been about deciding what path to follow, the path of her heart or the path of her mind. Shortly after I met her, Maya married a wonderful man and eventually found a job as a sales representative for a gourmet foods company. She quickly became very good at developing and nurturing clients and was soon making a good salary.

For some reason, I lost touch with Maya for a few months. When I finally got in touch with her husband, I found out that she was in the hospital and was very ill. I was shocked and immediately called her to see how she was doing. I could tell from the sound of her voice that things had not been going well. She was depressed, mentally and physically. When I asked her what she thought had caused her illness, she responded that it was the stress of her job that had brought on her physical collapse.

Maya got well, but it took a long time. After she recovered, she decided that she could not return to her former job. I don't know if at the outset of the next part of her journey as a Soul she consciously realized that she had been suffering because she was not allowing herself to follow her heart's path. But whether consciously or unconsciously driven, Maya was determined to do something that had some personal meaning to her.

Even though that something eluded her for what seemed like an eternity, ultimately she was led to the perfect opportunity which she expertly sculpted for herself to combine her passion for spirituality and music with her intellectual strengths. Maya now hosts a talk show on spirituality and creates magnificent guided meditations based on her dream imagery. Just last Friday night I went to hear her sing. I wonder where her heart and Soul will take her next...

THIRTEEN

CREATE A SPIRITUAL PLAN
FOR SUCCESS

As we have come to see in the course of the last three chapters, success is the result of knowledge and effort. In other words, when (1) we know that it is not some outside force but ourselves as Souls who are calling the shots in our lives; (2) we allow ourselves to have definite goals and aspirations; (3) we focus our attention and expend our energy on what we want; then (4) success is the end result.

With respect to work and career, success means knowing that you can get ahead on the job and then getting ahead; it means imagining your perfect job and then finding or creating it. With respect to life in general, success is understanding that you live in an abundant and beneficent universe and then using the law of cause and effect to fulfill all your material, emotional, and spiritual needs.

Success is a concept or an idea and not a physical thing. On the most profound of levels, it is freedom from fear. Many of us have not pursued success either because we are afraid that we aren't good enough to go after it or because we are afraid that we wouldn't be able to handle it if we were somehow able to achieve it. Those fears were well and good when we believed that we were bodies with brains/minds, but now that we know that we are Souls, immortal spiritual beings, sons and daughters of the divine, gods-in-the-making, these outmoded and limiting beliefs have no place whatsoever in our consciousness.

The time has come to leave fear behind. The time has come to combine knowledge with action. The time has come to first create and then live in the brave new world that we used to only dream about. The time has come to risk becoming successful. But first we need to make a plan. The following twelve steps are intended to help us do just that.

STEP 1: LISTENING

Sit quietly for a few moments. Relax your body and mind until you feel totally at peace. Immerse yourself in this feeling for as long as you can. Everything is perfect. Your life is perfect. You are perfectly healthy—physically, mentally, and spiritually. You are surrounded by the light of faith and love. Now, imagine yourself in a beautiful natural setting. You could be at the beach, in the mountains, by a lake, anywhere where you feel comfortable and peaceful. You are completely relaxed and happy. Silently, you ask your Soul to reveal to you what you need to know at the present moment, what you need to know as you begin this next leg of your spiritual journey. After a few moments, you are happy to hear the sound of your own voice speaking the following words to you:

It is no secret why you have chosen to read this book and others like it. You have always known that you are more than a mind and a body, that you are a spiritual being, that you are a Soul. You know that because you are first and foremost an eternal spiritual being; you were never born and will never die; therefore, no harm can ever come to you. Deep within you, you know that there is no reason to fear life.

You know that there are no accidents. You exist as a Soul in material reality for a reason. Every Soul is important and special. You are important and special. You are a part of the One Life of Spirit, of God, the creator of both the seen and the unseen realms. You are a co-creator with Spirit, the energy of life. You exist to explore the material universe, to express yourself within it, to create the world you want to live in. The energy of life is boundless and limitless. You are this energy.

Now that you know that you are a Soul, the only thing left for you to do is to allow what you have known for eternity on the cellular and unconscious levels to make a home in your conscious awareness. You simply need to trust your connection to the infinite good. You need only surrender to the infinite good. You are an agent of the infinite good. You live in an abundant universe. You are now and always have been successful. You know that what is God's is yours. Ask and you will receive.

STEP 2: ASKING AND RECEIVING

It is unfortunate, but because we aren't yet completely aware on the conscious level that we are Souls, we still spend most of our time complaining about all the things we want but don't have. Rarely do we sit down and focus our attention on the things we've asked for that we *have* received.

If we want to get into a success-oriented state of mind, we have to get in the habit of noticing when we get what we've asked for. In other words, we should make a concerted effort every single day to count our blessings and to take an inventory of the things we do have. When we begin to practice "abundant thinking"—that is, when we see ourselves as blessed by life, rather than cursed by it—a miraculous thing happens: we begin getting even more of what we want.

The following simple, quick, and painless exercises will get you started.

➤ Make a list of all the goals you set for your life from childhood up to the present that you have achieved. When I was a child, for example, I wanted to learn to speak French and live in Paris. I majored in French in college and lived in Paris my junior year. When I first moved to New York, I fell in love with Greenwich Village and vowed that I would someday live there. It took ten years, but I now live in the heart of the Village.

➤ Make a list of all the material things that you can remember ever having wanted that you received. (Christmas, Hanukkah, and birthday gifts count.) It doesn't matter how you received these things, whether someone gave them to you or you bought them for yourself. The point is: you asked and you received. This past year when my aunt Rosemary asked me what I wanted for Christmas, I told her that I wanted a food processor. Guess what? She gave me one. Yet another desire fulfilled.

STEP 3: SEEING IS BELIEVING

Like attracts like. According to the law of cause and effect, we are the cause, and the conditions of our lives are the effect. For

Spirit, there is no past or future. Everything takes place in the eternal now. Therefore, if we want to *be* successful, we have to *see* ourselves as successful *now*. The following exercise will get you on the right track.

➤ Using your imagination, write a detailed one-page description, in the present tense, of how you would think, act, and talk if you were the successful, spiritual person you want to be.

This exercise isn't as simple as it appears, is it? We may think that we want to be successful, but until we can really define not only what we mean by success, but also how success would affect our actions, our relationships, and our thoughts, we don't have much of a chance of achieving it.

If you find it difficult to complete this exercise, relax. For many people the word "success" is loaded with negative connotations, such as fear, greed, manipulative behavior, and so on. If this is the case for you, focus on any aspect of success that you feel comfortable manifesting now or think about what success *really* means to you. To me success means happiness. Therefore, I would write a one-page description of how I would think, talk, and act as a happy person. As I become comfortable with different aspects of success, I can always rewrite my description to include my new ideas. Life is a work in progress. You don't have to know or do everything today. Even one step in a positive direction can work miracles.

STEP 4: THINKING, TALKING, AND ACTING

Faith is the precondition of knowledge. By acting as if we already are what we want to become, or by acting as if we already have the thing we want to have, we are demonstrating faith in our ability to have the thing we want or to become the kind of person we yearn to be. When our intention and our actions are in perfect sync, Spirit lovingly responds, and our faith in the spiritual process is transformed into knowledge that the spiritual process works. When faith is transmuted into knowledge, we claim our power as co-creators with the source of our being.

The following exercise separates the thinkers from the doers. It is quite a different thing to talk about spirituality than it is to actually "work the work." Push past whatever resistance you may have to acting as if you are already successful and try the following exercise for one week.

➤ Suspend your disbelief and begin thinking, acting, and talking the way you described in Step 3. Keep a journal of how this new approach makes you feel and how it affects the way that other people react to you. Record any positive events that come as a result of this approach.

Do not be upset if you find this exercise nearly impossible to do. Keep at it until it gets easier. Do the exercise for as many weeks as necessary, until you notice that not only do you feel more positive about yourself, but also the world looks a lot more nurturing, benevolent, and beautiful.

Step 4 is not really an exercise, it's a way of life. If you can allow yourself to think, talk, and act successful even for a minute, you will get a glimpse of what is waiting for you on the other side of fear. The more you are able to faithfully concentrate on success, the less willing or able you will be to tolerate or encourage feelings of failure and self-doubt within yourself, and the more you will attract successful people and circumstances into your life. Once you are able to feel successful, material, emotional, and spiritual success is only a heartbeat away.

STEP 5: MAKING GOALS

If we have had the courage to take steps 1 through 4, we should have proven to ourselves by now that without a doubt our reality is *not* pre-established by some mysterious and dictatorial force or person out there somewhere, but *is* created by the thoughts we think, what we say, and how we act. This knowledge is the key to building the life we desire. With the knowledge that we are Souls who have the power of Spirit at our disposal, we can now begin to actualize some of our most heartfelt goals, dreams, and aspirations.

1. Divide a piece of paper into three columns. On the top of the first column, write "Short-Term Goals;" on the top of the second column write "Intermediate Goals;" and on the top of the third column write "Long-Term Goals."

2. Starting with the long-term goals column, write down one or two long-term career or material goals (take a look at your answer to Step 4 in Chapter 5), one or two long-term emotional or relationship-oriented goals (take a look at your answers to Step 3 in Chapter 9), and one or two long-term spiritual goals (take a look at your answer to Step 3 in Chapter 5) that you have for your life.

Long-term goals are those really big dreams you have for your life that are going to require time and effort in order to manifest. If you are now a senior in high school who dreams of becoming a professional singer-songwriter, for example, this dream is obviously a long-term career goal. Likewise, becoming a patient person or achieving total inner peace usually takes longer to achieve than attending a pottery class. Regardless of the nature of the specific goals you choose to pursue, make sure that the dreams you choose to actualize are ones that you really want to work on, not ones that others might be encouraging you to pursue. Remember, this plan for success is about your success, not about making anyone else happy.

3. Next, write down five intermediate career or material goals, five intermediate emotional or relationship-oriented goals, and five intermediate spiritual goals that would lead in the direction of fulfilling your long-term goals. An intermediate career goal for the high school student/singer would be to perform some songs that he or she had written for an audience. An intermediate emotional goal might be to get to the root of feelings of anger for a parent, and an intermediate spiritual goal might be to take a meditation class to learn how to quiet the mind.

4. Finally, write down ten short-term career or material goals, ten short-term emotional or relationship-oriented goals, and ten short-term spiritual goals that you can begin to work on now and that will lead you in the direction of fulfilling your intermediate goals. The student/singer might set joining the school choir, singing with a band, or taking voice lessons as a short-term career goal. One of his or her intermediate emotional goals might be to arrange for some psychotherapy or counseling to discuss his or her feelings of anger toward a parent, and one of his or her short-term spiritual goals might be to begin devoting a certain amount of time each day to reading spiritually oriented books or magazines.

STEP 6: TAKING ACTION

Now that we have proven to ourselves that we have the ability to think, talk, and act in a manner in keeping with our vision of success and we know what goals we would like to actualize, the time has come to take some action to demonstrate the earnestness of our desire.

➤ Pick one short-term career/material, one emotional/relationship, and one spiritual goal and take some action to make it a reality.

If for some reason it seems difficult to take some action with respect to the one goal you selected, or if the action you take doesn't seem to lead anywhere, you may not be ready for your goal to manifest in material reality just yet. That's okay. Simply reroute yourself and pick another goal that's easier to handle.

Several years ago I decided that it was time to pursue my goal of becoming a singer and I signed up for a group jazz voice class. Even though I was initially very excited, I dropped the class after only a few weeks. I felt like a failure for a few days until I realized that what I really needed was to take private voice lessons. Within a few weeks, a coworker recommended her voice teacher to me, and I ended up studying with him for many years. The key to success is to take small steps. It isn't always necessary to venture into the unknown. Walking into the unknown can be just as effective.

STEP 7: IMAGE-MAKING —PART ONE

Making images always reminds me how much I loved art class when I was in elementary school. No one expects a six-year-old to draw like Da Vinci, so at that age there is nothing holding you back from using your imagination to draw whatever you want, any way that you want. Even if the adults in your life have no idea what it is that you drew, that doesn't stop them from displaying your work on the refrigerator where you get to see it every day until a new picture takes its place.

The following exercise allows us to return to those days of fun and artistic freedom while impressing Spirit with a graphic representation of our goals at the same time.

➤ Create a scrapbook of pictures and photos that have personal meaning to you, which depict or symbolize the realization of the long-term career/material, emotional/relationship, and spiritual goals you have decided to actualize. Make sure to look at these pictures and/or photos several times a day, or if you are brave enough, display them on your refrigerator or anywhere else where you will see them many times during the day. If one of your career goals is to become a singer, for example, you could paint or draw yourself singing, or if you prefer, you could paste a photo of your head on the body of your favorite singer. Alternatively, you could create a collage of pictures of singers whom you admire and include photos of yourself in their company. If your long-term career goal is to become a CEO of a major corporation, you would include pictures of the kind of company you would like to manage and the industry you would like to work in, pictures of yourself in the company of other CEOs you admire, or a drawing of a ladder (to symbolize the corporate ladder) with your picture at the very top.

The key to this exercise is to let yourself go, to allow yourself to create the image that best suits you. You don't have to show your scrapbook to anyone else, and no one else has to understand what your pictures mean or why you are drawing or creating them. Keep in mind that your scrapbook is for you to express yourself as a Soul. Your intention is to communicate what you want to Spirit, not to win the approval of friends or family or to win an art contest.

STEP 8: IMAGE-MAKING—PART TWO

In Step 3, we created a detailed description of the successful person we envisioned ourselves to be. In Chapter 11, we learned how to write an image to get a job we would love. Now it's time to use the same technique to actualize our long-term material, emotional, and spiritual goals.

➤ Using your imagination, write a detailed description in the present tense of exactly what your life would be like when your long-term goals become reality. It's important to set the right tone for your description; in order to get in the right mood, start off with your mission statement from Chapter 5. At the end of your description, practice abundant thinking by thanking Life or Spirit or God for all that you have and for all that will be given to you. Let's take our student/singer who is aspiring to become a patient, peaceful person as an example. His or her image would look something like this:

> I am first and foremost a spiritual being. My life is meaningful and has purpose. I am a Soul and have the power to change negative circumstances into positive opportunities at will. With faith, love, hope, duty, compassion, patience, and kindness, I pursue my spiritual

objective, which is to evolve spiritually each and every day and to generously assist others to fulfill their dreams and aspirations. My relationships with my family, especially my parents, are blessed by Spirit and continue to evolve in and grow in love, forgiveness, and compassion. Two of the greatest loves in my life are music and singing. I am so happy as a professional singer and songwriter. My CD, which contains songs I cowrote with my wonderful musical partner, is extremely well received by the critics and the general public. I love being a recording artist as well as singing in live performances. The musicians in my band are very talented and share my musical vision. I have an unrelenting enthusiasm for music and for my audience. All my material, emotional, and spiritual needs are generously and abundantly fulfilled by Spirit. I am thankful and grateful for all the many gifts and blessings in my life now and for those I am about to receive. Thank you, Life.

STEP 9: AFFIRMING

While writing your image goes a long way toward redirecting your energy in the direction you want to go in, it doesn't go far enough. As we said in Chapter 11, repetition is the key to success. Over the years, your mind has been conditioned to believe that you won't get what you want out of life or that even if it's possible to get what you want, the process will be long and arduous, requiring many sacrifices along the way. If we want to turn over power to our Souls to direct our lives, we have to affirm loudly and clearly to ourselves over and over what exactly it is that we want, until the mind's old conditioning has less and less power over our thoughts and our actions.

➤ Read your image aloud to yourself three times a day for at least sixty days, and once a day thereafter indefinitely. As you read it, immerse yourself in the feelings that surface as a result of knowing that your dreams will come true.

STEP 10: VISUALIZING

➤ Sit quietly in a chair right after you wake up in the morning and right before you go to bed at night. Close your eyes and slowly breathe in and out until you feel calm and relaxed. Clear your mind of any unwanted thoughts and distractions. Develop a clear mental picture of the success you want to achieve. See yourself as you would look, and allow yourself to feel how you would feel, having achieved your goals. Hold on to the image for as long as you can.

STEP 11: MANIFESTING

The time it takes for your long-term goals to manifest varies based on the degree of faith or knowledge you have, the earnestness of your desire, and your ability to act on your own behalf. Remember, Spirit or God is in charge of the universe; but as a Soul you have the power of the universe at your disposal. When all the conditions necessary for the manifestation of your dreams are in place, they will come true. While you are waiting:

➤ Keep the faith.
➤ Take action until all of your short-term and intermediate goals have been achieved. Then start the process all over again by first creating and then achieving new short-term and inter-

mediate goals, until your long-term dreams have been actu-
alized.

➤ Do everything possible within your power to help others to
actualize their dreams.

STEP 12: ACCEPTING

When our goals, aspirations, and dreams serve Life, rather than
threaten or destroy it, everything is possible. We can achieve anything we set out to achieve. We can be whatever we want to be
and live the life we love. We can partake of the abundance of
the universe. We can ask, knowing that in due time we will
receive. When we recognize our true nature as living Souls and
act accordingly, when we pursue what makes us happy, we are
graciously accepting the gift of Life. Whether we know it or not,
that's all Life has ever wanted us to do.

PART FIVE

THE END IS ALWAYS THE BEGINNING

*The multiplicity of things we have become
through time; all the things we strive to be.
I wonder, hope and ponder that there be
no conflict between past, present and future
of our dreams; rather let them be met and welcome;
let there always be mysteries to enrapture.*

—MIROSLAW KUCHARSKI

FOURTEEN

TRAVELING THE ROAD TO COSMIC CONSCIOUSNESS

There is no doubt that we are currently in the midst of a revolution. But unlike revolutions of the past, this one is not taking place on a battlefield or in the streets. Rather, it is taking place deep within each and every one of us as we struggle to overcome our lower natures and align ourselves with our Souls, with Spirit, with God. Until recently only the very courageous dared to join this revolution in consciousness; only a few evolved Souls dared to seek the Truth and to live in accordance with it. Now, however, thanks to the fearless pioneers who have ventured into the uncharted spiritual wilderness in advance of the rest of us, the spiritual path is illuminated, and we can all find our way home.

Despite the apocalyptic predictions of those who presume to know the deepest thoughts of the Creator, humankind is evolving. A faint memory of our spiritual heritage and a small yet unrelenting desire to reconnect with our source lies dormant within each of our hearts and Souls. It makes no difference whether it takes moments or decades to liberate this hidden memory or to act upon this desire. Because we are all individual manifestations of Spirit, success is assured for everyone. It is impossible for even one of us to be left outside the great circle of Life. However, while it is inevitable that we will all get to the promised land, the path we choose to take and the quality of our journey is completely up to us.

We have traveled a great distance. But our spiritual quest is far from over. The end is always the beginning. Thanks to the magnificent cosmic law of cause and effect, every moment is an opportunity to set a whole new life in motion. The possibility of rebirth is present every second. Contrary to popular opinion, it is never too late to change. Nor is it ever too soon to embrace the knowledge that we are not minds and bodies but spiritual beings who need not fear death, failure, or abandonment. We can align ourselves with the power of Life by allowing the Spirit within to express itself as joy, happiness, faith, love, hope, kindness, generosity, compassion, duty, and patience. We can consciously choose to serve Life, and consequently ourselves, by acting as Souls, as agents of the ultimate good, regardless of the circumstances or the other people with which we seem to be confronted, even in that most difficult of environments, the workplace.

Prior to acquiring spiritual knowledge, *to work* means *to make a living*; that is, to make money. With spiritual knowledge, however, *to work* means simply *to express ourselves as living Souls*. We express ourselves as Souls when we allow ourselves to trust the all-present, all-powerful, and all-knowing energy or force that is Life. We express ourselves as spiritual beings when we allow faith rather than fear to guide us as we pursue that which brings us and gives others the most pleasure. Because we are made in the image and likeness of the consciousness that designed and created the universe, our lives have meaning. Therefore, any job that we do and any work that we perform is meaningful.

Our beliefs create our reality. Therefore, if we want to change or improve any aspect of our lives, including our work lives, we have to be willing to change our beliefs. If we want to be the masters of our own destinies we must change our belief in the illusion of many lives, to a belief in the One Life. Energy/God/Spirit is all that exists. Our material reality is simply the reflection of our spiritual reality. When we shift our awareness from the material to the spiritual, we find what we have been seeking so desperately—peace, safety, and security—and are no longer the slaves of our external surroundings, no longer the victims of other people, places, situations, or things. When we dedicate our lives to expressing the beauty of Spirit, we see the truth that exists beyond the relative states of good and bad, we feel the essence of life radiating within and outside of us, we rise above the confusion and chaos that was once our reality, and are able to create the life of our dreams.

The spiritual path is the most direct road to success. But if we want to see results, we must commit ourselves body, mind, and Soul to a new way of life. We must have the courage to venture into the unknown. We must get out of our heads and trust the wisdom of our hearts. We must push past our resistance and base our lives on a principle, a code of ethics, a philosophy of life that is inclusive, not exclusive, and which promotes abundance rather than lack, cooperation rather than competition.

When we commit to the inner life, we give up our attachment to the fads and fashions of the external world. We give up the false belief that it is the clothes that we wear, the car we drive, the amount of money we have in the bank, the level of education we have acquired, or our job title that determines our worth. We are children of the universe. We are instruments of the divine. We are aspects of God, and God's worth cannot be measured.

God is infinite. There is plenty for everyone. We need not resent another person's good fortune. We can have and be anything that we want. We can live the life we yearn to live. When out of jealousy, envy, or fear we stand in the way of another person's success, we inhibit our own progress. There is only One Life. Whenever one of God's creatures succeeds, we all take another step farther along the path.

Sometimes after we have decided to commit ourselves to a new approach to life, our minds and egos, which we have relied on for many years to guide our actions, have no other choice but to test the strength of our conviction by placing us right in the middle of some very trying or negative situations. When this occurs, we must not confuse kindness with weakness. By turning the other cheek and loving those who hate us, we are affirming our allegiance to a higher power, we are living in accordance with a nobler and more exacting law than any created by humankind—the law of karma. What we put into Life is what we receive from Life. Therefore, revenge is never sweet. When we commit ourselves to the spiritual path we anchor ourselves to the positive and let the chips fall where they may, knowing that because energy/Spirit cannot be created or destroyed, no harm can come to us. We remain resolute in our decision to act as Souls, knowing that eventually our egos will give up the fight and we will be reborn in Spirit.

As anyone who has ever tried to live as a Soul can attest, traveling the spiritual path can sometimes be a lonely journey. Even though the path can only be traveled alone, becoming a member of a spiritual community or following a spiritual course of study with other like-minded individuals can make staying on the path much easier. It is helpful, especially at the beginning, to be able to share our thoughts and experiences with other people with whom we feel comfortable. While it is well worth the effort, if happiness or success in any way, shape, or form is our goal, it isn't easy to let go of our old way of thinking. Sometimes the process can be joyfully liberating, while at other times it can be difficult and painful. It is at those times when the old conditioning appears to be winning that talking to someone who shares our philosophy of life can give us the inspiration we need to stay the course.

Acquiring spiritual knowledge is no different from acquiring any other kind of knowledge. Patience is required. Anyone who decides to learn to play the piano doesn't expect to sit down and play a Chopin sonata after only one or two lessons. Just as it takes time, dedication, and practice to become an accomplished pianist, it takes time, dedication, and practice to become a self-actualized Soul. Even the Buddha didn't become enlightened overnight. He spent many years seeking the answers to life's mysteries, sometimes even going down the wrong road, before he found the way out of the cycle of suffering and rebirth.

There is no doubt that we will make many mistakes in our quest for spiritual understanding. Even after we commit ourselves to the spiritual path, it is inevitable that we will revert back to our old way of doing things a thousand times a day or more. The key to success, however, is not to avoid making mistakes or slipping off the path, but to be compassionate and forgiving with ourselves when we do. This may just be the most challenging part of the entire process of spiritual unfolding.

Most of us treat ourselves far worse than our worst enemies could ever conceive of treating us. We have become masters of self-cruelty, self-hatred, and guilt. Every day we criticize ourselves needlessly for little mistakes and use harsh and destructive words such as stupid, ugly, untalented, and unlovable to describe ourselves. Then, to make matters worse, we trivialize our strengths and deny ourselves the right to pursue happiness. As a result of this insane self-cruelty, we cannot help but see the world as violent, unsafe, and barren. We feel that we have no other choice but to pursue career paths not in keeping with our desires. We can't help but enter into unsuitable and destructive relationships. Worst of all, we find ourselves insisting that our children follow in our footsteps, even when we are well aware that those footsteps lead only to pain and suffering.

We must stop this self-destructive thinking and behavior if we want to achieve the happiness, peace, and success we deserve as living Souls. We have every right to the best Life has to offer. There is no reason why each and every one of us can't pursue the career we want to pursue, have enough money to live comfortably, and still have plenty of time to nurture and support our children, our spouses, our friends, and everyone else with whom we come in contact on a daily basis. There is no reason why everyone can't win. If we want to be successful and prosperous, we must first give ourselves permission to feel successful and prosperous. If we want to receive compassion, mercy, and forgiveness from others, we must first be compassionate, merciful, and forgiving with ourselves. If we want to heal the planet, we must first heal ourselves.

The good news is that by recognizing that we are Souls, eternal spiritual beings, we have already taken a giant step toward self-healing. Now, we need only think, talk, and act successful if we want to be successful. We need only love ourselves if we want to feel God's love. We need only take one small step on the spiritual path every day to create heaven on earth.

As we travel the road to cosmic consciousness we need only remember:

> ➤ Energy/God/Spirit is all that exists.
> ➤ There are no people, places, situations, or things.
> ➤ We are living Souls, agents of Spirit, instruments of the divine.
> ➤ Perception is reality. The cause is the same as the effect. If we want positive situations to manifest in our lives, we need only

look for the positive in everyone and every situation we encounter and go about performing positive actions.

➤ Ask and we shall receive.

Life does not have to be an endless cycle of pain. It can be a moving meditation—a never-ending dialogue with God. The spiritual journey begins and ends with the self. There is only One Life—and you are it.

APPENDIX A

DEFINITION OF TERMS

SOUL: Many schools of spirituality see the Soul as the immaterial part of the living entity that survives bodily death. These schools view human beings as bodies and minds who have a Soul. In this book, which is heavily influenced by the philosophy of *Concept-Therapy*® (see Introduction), Soul is defined as the true nature of the living entity and as the co-ordinator of both the body and the mind. Simply put, we are not minds and bodies that happen to have a Soul, we are living Souls whose minds and bodies are expressions of the Soul's essence.

In the context of this book, Soul can also be viewed as the "higher self." As living Souls, we are ever-evolving entities and "agents of Spirit" who are connected to "all that is."

INTUITION: The faculty that develops within the individual as one learns to access the Soul. The faculty that communicates information from the Soul to the mind and body.

MIND: The activity of the brain. Conditioned by experience in material reality and ruled by negative emotion. Also known as the ego.

SPIRIT: Spirit is a synonym for energy, Universal Consciousness, Chi, Nature, or God, and is all-present, all-powerful, and all-knowing. The law governing Spirit is the same as the law that governs energy, i.e., energy or Spirit can neither be created nor destroyed; it can only move and change. Energy or Spirit is the animating force of both the seen and the unseen realms that make up the entire universe; in fact, it is life itself.

When Spirit is channeled through the Soul and not the mind, positive, life-affirming situations manifest in material reality, and the Soul is propelled to higher levels of awareness on the spiritual level.

ONE LIFE PRINCIPLE: As individual living Souls, we are directly linked to one another through Spirit and are manifestations of Spirit. Spirit is Life itself; therefore, it is the only Life there is.

LAW OF KARMA (LAW OF CAUSE AND EFFECT): While often seen as the law that governs the reincarnation process, the law of karma operates every moment of every day, as it is simply the law of cause and effect. Each thought we think or act we perform is a cause that creates an equal effect. If we think and express positive emotion, the effect will be that the situations we encounter will be positive and life affirming. If we think and express negative emotion, we will encounter situations that are negative and destructive.

RIGHT THINKING: The process of accessing and expressing the positive emotions of the Soul.

RIGHT ACTION: The process of performing acts that are in keeping with one's true nature as a living Soul.

TRANSMUTATION OF ENERGY: Energy can only move and change; therefore, as living Souls we have the power through our thoughts and our actions to transform negative energy into positive energy at will. Since the past cannot be changed, and the future is yet to unfold, this power exists only in the present moment.

APPENDIX B

OVERVIEW OF THE NEGATIVE AND POSITIVE EMOTIONAL STATES

MIND	SOUL
Principle Emotional State: **FEAR**	Principle Emotional State: **FAITH**
Fear is an emotional state of the mind. It results from the *belief* that we are separate from Spirit/God. The underlying assumption behind the emotional state of fear is that the universe is not inherently good and that "all is not well." This negative conditioning shapes and molds our reality, e.g., our fear of failure makes us fail, our fear of missing a deadline creates the conditions that may cause us to miss a deadline.	Faith is an emotional state of the Soul. It results from the *belief* that we are all living Souls, individual manifestations of Spirit/God. The underlying assumption behind the emotional state of faith is that the universe is inherently good and that "all is well." Faith is the precondition of knowledge, e.g., if we have faith that a thing will manifest, then once it does manifest, we *know* that the process works.
FEAR manifests itself in:	**FAITH** manifests itself in:
GREED: An unending selfish desire for more than one needs. Fear that there is not enough to go around and that we will not get our share.	**KINDNESS**: To show endless mercy, charity, and generosity. Faith/knowledge that we live in an abundant universe with plenty to go around.
WORRY: Anxiety, apprehension. Fear that "bad things" will happen or that we will not be able to handle the situations we encounter.	**HOPE**: A belief in a positive outcome. Faith/knowledge in ultimate goodness and the belief that everything will turn out for the best.
ANGER: Extreme hostility, indignation, or exasperation. Fear that we will not be able to control a situation.	**PATIENCE**: Peaceful, calm perseverance. Faith/knowledge that we can handle any situation we are confronted with.
JEALOUSY: Resentment regarding another person's success or advantages. Fear of not receiving adequate attention and of losing what one has.	**DUTY**: To take personal responsibility and to fulfill one's spiritual mission or calling. Faith/knowledge that Spirit/God has our best interests at heart.

CRITICISM: Disapproval or judgment of another person or one's self. Fear of not being satisfied.	COMPASSION: To show approval, mercy, and nonjudgment. Faith/knowledge that all of our needs are being satisfied.
HATRED: Violent hostility or animosity. Intense fear of another or of a situation. Fear and hatred are the most powerful of the negative emotional states.	LOVE: Unselfish, generous affection and warmth. Faith/knowledge of the oneness of all life. Faith and love are the most powerful of the positive emotional states/spiritual principles.